DOMESTIC VIOLENCE, CRIME [illegible] VICTIMS ACT 2004

Related titles by Law Society Publishing

Criminal Justice Act 2003

A Guide to the New Law
Andrew Keogh
1–85328–877–2

Sexual Offences Act 2003

A Guide to the New Law
Paul Lewis
1–85328–965–5

CLSA Duty Solicitor's Handbook (2nd edition)

Andrew Keogh
1–85328–975–2

Forensic Practice in Criminal Cases

Lynne Townley and Roger Ede
1–85328–821–7

DOMESTIC VIOLENCE, CRIME AND VICTIMS ACT 2004

A Guide to the New Law

Claire Bessant

The Law Society

ISBN 1–85328–902–7

Published in 2005 by the Law Society
113 Chancery Lane, London WC2A 1PL

Typeset by J&L Composition, Filey, North Yorkshire
Printed by TJ International Ltd, Padstow, Cornwall

CONTENTS

PREFACE

The Domestic Violence, Crime and Victims Act 2004 bears little resemblance to the Bill presented to Parliament in December 2003. As recognised by Baroness Anelay of St Johns:

> This appears now to be less of a domestic violence Bill than a general crime Bill. The serious nature of that is simply that, when practitioners seek to find particular legislation, they will not necessarily direct themselves to this Bill as the source of that information, because it is being referred to in a general sense simply as the Domestic Violence Bill. (House of Lords, Hansard, col. 1423, 11 March 2004)

The Act is intended to provide greater protection for victims of domestic violence, and it is certainly hoped that it will do so. Concerns have been raised, however, that the amendments to the Family Law Act 1996 and the Protection from Harassment Act 1997 place excessive emphasis on punishment. They may remove the victim's ability to pursue a remedy through the civil courts. Further guidance on the interaction between the civil and criminal courts is essential.

Whilst concerns are raised about increased criminalisation of domestic violence law, it is hoped that the much welcomed introduction of the Commissioner for Victims and Witnesses, statutory Victims Advisory Panel and Code of Practice will promote a cultural change in the criminal justice system, benefiting all victims of criminal offences.

Those who oppose diminishment of the role of the jury, should note that juries no longer have power to determine whether a defendant is unfit to plead or not guilty by reason of insanity. Their role is diminished in cases where an offender has committed multiple offences. The new offence of homicide where one or more individuals has either caused or allowed the death of a child or vulnerable adult is believed by many to be drafted too widely. The combined effect of section 5 of the Act, together with procedural amendments introduced by section 6, is not merely to ensure that convictions under section 5 are obtained. The government also hope to provoke the less culpable co-defendant into giving evidence against the other, evidence which may be used to obtain a conviction for murder or manslaughter.

I have attempted to explain the key provisions of this Act in some detail whilst still producing a book of manageable size. This book is intended to be both interesting and useful to the busy practitioner. The full Act is provided in the Appendix, for those who wish to read its tortuous detail.

This text takes account of the law as at 10 December 2004. Since regulations and rules must still be made before the Act is fully implemented, this text can, unfortunately, provide only an introduction to how the Act is likely to operate in practice.

My final words must go to my husband, Paul Cowie, and my parents, Vin and Petrea Bessant. I am hugely grateful to them all, for their assistance with this text, but more importantly for their support.

TABLE OF CASES

TABLE OF STATUTES

TABLE OF SECONDARY AND EUROPEAN LEGISLATION

SECONDARY LEGISLATION

EUROPEAN LEGISLATION

PART I DOMESTIC VIOLENCE, CRIME AND VICTIMS ACT 2004

1 AN OVERVIEW OF THE ACT

Key points:

- Background to the Domestic Violence, Crime and Victims Act 2004.
- Overview of the key provisions of the Act, by area:
  - domestic violence and harassment;
  - amendments to criminal law;
  - greater rights for victims and witnesses.
- What is not included within the Act.
- Implementation.

1.1 INTRODUCTION

Baroness Scotland of Asthal began the Domestic Violence, Crime and Victim Bill's second reading stating:

> The Bill represents the most radical overhaul of domestic violence legislation in 30 years. It reflects the fact that domestic violence is unacceptable, that victims must be protected and offenders punished. (House of Lords, Hansard, col. 949, 15 December 2003)

The Bill as initially introduced in the House of Lords implemented many of the amendments to criminal and civil law suggested in *Safety and Justice: The Government's Proposals on Domestic Violence*, Home Office (July 2003). More than one-third of the Bill initially focused upon victims and witnesses, implementing the promises given by the government in *A New Deal for Victims and Witnesses: National Strategy to Deliver Improved Services*, Home Office (July 2003). Criminal law amendments were otherwise limited to the introduction of a new homicide offence and a two-stage trial applying in cases of multiple offending. Both of these provisions responded to Law Commission consultations, which resulted in recommendations for legislation (*Children: Their Non-Accidental Death or Serious Injury (Criminal Trials)*, Law Commission Report 282

(September 2003) and *The Effective Prosecution of Multiple Offending*, Law Commission Report 277 (October 2002)).

Significant amendments have been made during the Bill's progress through Parliament. The Domestic Violence, Crime and Victims Act 2004 ('the Act') can no longer be considered a 'domestic violence' Act. The Act now clearly reflects the government's wider strategy for bringing offenders to justice.

The large majority of the criminal law amendments, many of which amend existing Acts, were introduced only after the Bill had passed to the House of Commons. By the time the Bill returned to the House of Lords for consideration of these amendments, the Lords had little option but to accept the Bill as it stood.

The provisions concerning the new offence of homicide, and the changes this will make to evidence and procedure, were debated at length. Upon conclusion of the debates, concerns about procedural amendments introduced by section 6 of the Act remained evident. The dilution of the jury's powers, with the introduction of the two-stage procedure in cases of multiple offending, and the provisions permitting determination of fitness to plead by a judge, remain equally contentious.

1.1.1 Composition of the Act

The Act itself is composed of three parts, comprising 63 sections and 12 schedules.

The provisions within the Act can be divided into three groups:

- amendments to civil and criminal provisions regarding domestic violence;
- amendments to criminal law and procedure in England, Wales and Northern Ireland and upon court-martial;
- measures affording increased support and assistance to victims and witnesses of criminal offences and anti-social behaviour.

1.1.2 This text

The purpose of this book is to provide an overview of the main provisions, together with an explanation of how they will operate in practice. The Act amends certain facets of the law relating to Northern Ireland and to court-martial but this text considers only those provisions relating to England and Wales.

1.2 CONTENTS OF THE ACT

1.2.1 Domestic violence and harassment

Amendments are made to the Family Law Act 1996 to extend its protection to same sex couples and, to a more limited extent, to non-cohabiting couples who have had an intimate relationship of significant duration. The problem that all victims do not have equal access to protection because of legal differences in their relationship is not addressed. Distinctions between the duration of occupation orders made in favour of spouses and those made in favour of cohabitants remain.

The police and criminal courts are both granted greater power to ensure that those who harass or assault cannot easily escape arrest or punishment. At a time when the government is legislating to introduce multi-agency domestic violence homicide reviews to enable lessons to be learned from domestic homicides, it is surprising that the effect of this Act is to raise, not answer, questions about the role of the law in protecting the victim of domestic violence. Whilst more domestic violence cases seem likely to come within criminal jurisdiction, criminal courts are not obliged to enquire into the existence of civil orders. They do not need to address concerns about the victim's housing and child contact. Criminal courts do not need to consider the views of the victim, who will not be party to the proceedings. In *Lomas* v. *Parle* [2004] 1 WLR 1642, Thorpe LJ suggested that the Domestic Violence, Crime and Victims Bill would provide an opportunity to reconsider the current dual system, information-sharing by the courts and the possibility of an integrated court. Whilst a Working Party has been established to examine the relationship between the criminal and family jurisdictions, and to consider integrated courts, the Act simply ignores these issues.

1.2.2 Amendments to criminal law and procedure

A number of amendments are introduced to implement the conclusions of consultations undertaken by the Law Commission and/or to implement government strategies both to bring more offenders to justice and to require those offenders to contribute towards reparation for their victims:

1. Section 5 introduces a new offence of homicide, designed to address the problems highlighted in *R* v. *Lane and Lane* (1986) 82 Cr. App. R 5 The offence is drafted widely to catch members of the household in which the deceased lived and those, such as boyfriends, who visited frequently. The prosecution must show that the defendant killed the deceased, or that a defendant who ought to have foreseen risk to the deceased failed to take reasonable steps to prevent the death. Concerns are raised about the ability of those who are mentally impaired, or too afraid to act, to meet such tests. Procedural amendments introduced, to apply in cases where the section 5 offence is jointly charged with charges of murder and manslaughter, are particularly criticised for removing the prosecution's obligation to present a *prima facie* case for murder. The result of section 5 and section 6 together is to present an unenviable choice to the defendant: fail to give evidence, thereby risking adverse inferences and a prosecution on the section 5 offence, or risk giving evidence which may bolster a weak prosecution case for murder or manslaughter. The government's ultimate aim appears to be to provoke the less culpable defendant into giving evidence, which can then be used to convict more defendants of murder.
2. A two-stage procedure is introduced to replace the practice of charging offences as specimens of a wider range of offending, disapproved of in *R* v.

Kidd and others [1998] 1 WLR 604. It is intended to ensure that defendants receive punishment for the totality of their offending, but that they are not sentenced for offences which they have not admitted or for which they have not been convicted. Permitting certain counts within an indictment to be tried without a jury is considered by some to be an assault on jury trial. 'Safeguards' introduced to ensure that the defendant still receives a fair trial were, however, considered to be sufficient by the Joint Committee on Human Rights. Liberty, nevertheless, considers that the condition, requiring a trial of certain counts without a jury to take place when 'in the interests of justice', can never be met. The Law Commission's proposal to widen use of compound allegations to offending other than theft or fraud is not addressed by the Act, although it is suggested by the Attorney-General, Lord Goldsmith (House of Lords, Hansard, col. 1426, 11 March 2004) that extension of these principles to offending other than theft or fraud might be achieved by a change in the Indictment Rules 1971, SI 1971/1253, if the government so desired.

3. Resources for the Victims' Fund, shortly to be established, will come from payments recovered from offenders; from surcharges levied on criminal convictions and penalty notices, and from the recovery of criminal injuries compensation from offenders. The provisions requiring road traffic offenders to pay a surcharge to victims of crime if they break the speed limit twice in three years, so contentious when suggested in *Compensation and Support for Victims of Crime*, Home Office (January 2004), seem likely to remain contentious.
4. The jury's role is reduced further by sections 22 and 23, which remove from the jury's remit power to determine whether a defendant is fit to plead, or not guilty by reason of insanity. The courts' new power to make a hospital order for defendants who are unfit or insane, which ensures that no admission to hospital may be ordered unless the defendant is mentally disordered and requires treatment, is, however, to be welcomed.
5. Further provisions relating to mentally disordered offenders, introduced at the last moment, appropriately extend rights to make representations and receive information both to victims of offenders who have been imprisoned and to victims of offenders subject to a Mental Health Act 1983 disposal.
6. The extended powers granted to civilian enforcement officers, agencies appointed by magistrates' courts and to magistrates' courts, to ensure effective enforcement of warrants and as to community penalties, reflect, much as the rest of the Bill now does, the government's aim to ensure 'justice' – or punishment and recompense.

1.2.3 Victims and witnesses

The main concern about the numerous, very welcome, provisions introduced to provide support to victims and witnesses is their lack of real power. Whilst it is hoped that introduction of the Code of Practice for Victims and appointment of the Commissioner for Victims and Witnesses will bring a cultural change, particularly within the criminal justice system, victims still have no enforceable rights.

1.2.4 Omissions from the Act

A noticeable omission from the Act is a definition of domestic violence. Without a uniform definition, many agencies argue it is simply not possible to assess how prevalent domestic violence is. Whilst the issue is being considered by the Domestic Violence Ministerial Working Group, one cannot help but agree with Lord Thomas of Gresford that:

> It is curious to have it called Domestic Violence, Crime and Victims Bill, without anyone having a clear idea how far domestic violence extends; who may be parties to domestic violence; who may not be; what type of conduct is regarded as domestic violence and whether it covers psychological harm. (House of Lords, Hansard, col. 1218, 9 March 2004)

The register of civil orders proposed at paragraphs 57–59 of *Safety and Justice: The Government's Proposals on Domestic Violence*, Home Office (June 2003), which would permit police and prosecutors to check easily a suspect's history, is not mentioned in the Act. It appears, however, that the police national computer is likely to be used to establish a central register (Parliamentary Under-Secretary of State for the Home Department, Paul Goggins, House of Commons, Hansard, col. 403, 22 June 2004).

The law relating to contact between children and parents in cases of domestic violence is not amended. Whilst subject to considerable debate, no further amendments are being made to the law to assist those individuals who suffer domestic violence from their partner and who are subject to immigration control. Specific support for victims of domestic violence through the institution of national advocacy services is not included. Whilst a matter of some debate, no extension has been made to the category of witnesses eligible for assistance on grounds of fear or distress about testifying.

Also missing is any reference to a change to the law on provocation, to enable women in violent situations to rely on the defence of provocation and to prevent men from relying on minimal provocation where they have lost self-control and killed. The government were unwilling to legislate to amend the current law before the Law Commission reports.

1.3 IMPLEMENTATION

The Act will be implemented in stages, by commencement order, starting from March 2005, with secondary implementation likely to commence in summer 2005. It is hoped that during the course of 2005 the majority of the Bill will be implemented. The timetable itself is dependent on availability of resources, introduction of secondary legislation and new training requirements.

It is anticipated that the new section 5 offence and related procedural changes, together with provisions relating to fitness to plead and concerning common assault, will be introduced first. Whilst provisions regarding disclosure orders are likely to be implemented relatively quickly, additional training may be required prior to implementation of the other enforcement provisions.

The amendments to the Family Law Act 1996, to the Protection from Harassment Act 1997 and provisions permitting victims of violent and sexual offences to make representations and receive information will have some resource implications, and are unlikely to come into force before summer 2005.

The provisions relating to trial by jury of sample counts cannot be implemented until new Rules of Court are drafted and the provisions regarding prosecution appeals have been implemented.

The Traffic Bill may delay implementation of surcharges for road traffic offenders. Amendments to the Criminal Injuries Compensation Act 1995 cannot be implemented until the Scottish Parliament introduces its own comparable legislation, and detailed secondary legislation is prepared.

The draft Code of Practice for Victims is likely to be published for consultation in January 2005. It is anticipated that the Code of Practice will come into force in December 2005, and that extension to the powers of the Parliamentary Ombudsman, and sections relating to disclosure of information will be implemented at the same time. The Commissioner for Victims and Witnesses should be formally appointed late in 2005.

PART II **DOMESTIC VIOLENCE AND HARASSMENT**

2 DOMESTIC VIOLENCE AND HARASSMENT: AN INTRODUCTION

The provisions detailed in Chapters 3 to 6 have been introduced to address problems identified following government consultation in *Safety and Justice: The Government's Proposals on Domestic Violence*, Home Office (July 2003). They reflect the second strand of the government's strategy for domestic violence – protection and justice.

Chapters 3 to 5 detail those provisions that amend the Family Law Act 1996, the Protection from Harassment Act 1997 and the law relating to common assault. The aim of these provisions is to maximise protection for all victims, ensure an effective police response when domestic violence is reported, and to stop violence recurring.

In Chapter 6 the provisions introducing statutory domestic homicide reviews are briefly explained.

3 AMENDMENTS TO THE FAMILY LAW ACT 1996

Key points:

- Breach of non-molestation order to be a criminal offence.
- Consequential amendments made to provisions regarding non-molestation orders, powers of arrest and undertakings.
- Associated persons to include:
  - individuals who have had an intimate personal relationship of significant duration;
  - first cousins.
- Cohabitants includes same sex couples.

3.1 BACKGROUND

Sections 1 to 4 of the Act were introduced to resolve the following concerns identified in *Safety and Justice: The Government's Proposals on Domestic Violence*, Home Office (July 2003) paragraphs 38–50:

- people in a relationship who have never lived together may not have access to non-molestation orders under the Family Law Act (FLA) 1996, s.42;
- the definition of cohabiting couples excludes same sex couples: this limits their ability to apply for occupation orders;
- enforcement by the police depends upon attachment of a power of arrest to the non-molestation order.

An additional concern, that the FLA 1996 did not make clear whether the court had power to issue an arrest warrant following breach of an undertaking, is also addressed.

3.2 NON-MOLESTATION ORDERS

A non-molestation order may be made:

(a) upon application by a person who is associated with the respondent (FLA 1996, s.42(2)(a));
(b) when, in any family proceedings to which the respondent is a party, the court considers a non-molestation order should be made for the benefit of any other party to the proceedings or any relevant child (FLA 1996, s.42(2)(b));
(c) the court is also obliged expressly to consider whether to exercise its power to make a non-molestation order of its own volition, when it is asked to make an occupation order (FLA 1996, s.42(4A) as inserted by Sched. 10, para. 36 to the Act).

The applicant for the purpose of section 42 means either the person who made the application for an order, or the person in whose favour the court has exercised its powers (FLA 1996, s.42(4B) as inserted by Sched. 10, para. 36 to the Act).

3.3 BREACH OF NON-MOLESTATION ORDER TO BE A CRIMINAL OFFENCE

3.3.1 The offence

Section 1 of the Act inserts a new section 42A into the FLA 1996, which provides that where any person, without reasonable excuse, does anything that he is prohibited from doing by a non-molestation order, they are guilty of an offence (FLA 1996, s.42A(1)). The offence may be prosecuted either in the magistrates' court or the Crown Court.

'Reasonable excuse'

The respondent who due to disability, blindness or illiteracy is not aware of, or does not understand the terms of, a non-molestation order, may be able to rely upon the defence of 'reasonable excuse' for breaching the order.

Without notice orders

Where the non-molestation order is made 'without notice' under FLA 1996, s.45(1), the respondent will not be guilty of the new offence unless the conduct which contravenes the non-molestation order took place 'when he was aware of the existence of the order' (FLA 1996, s.42A(2)).

The provision does not require the respondent to have seen the order or to be aware of the detail of its terms. This ensures that a respondent who has deliberately evaded service of a non-molestation order may still be arrested and prosecuted for its breach.

Breach of occupation order not a criminal offence

A history of violence or molestation is not a prerequisite for the grant of an occupation order. The decision has, therefore, been made not to make breach of an occupation order a criminal offence.

3.3.2 The penalty

The new offence attracts a much higher maximum penalty than the maximum sentence for contempt, of two years.

If a person is found guilty of an offence under FLA 1996, s.42A then they will be liable on conviction on indictment to imprisonment for a term not exceeding five years, or a fine, or both (FLA 1996, s.42A(5)(a)). If a person is found guilty of such an offence on summary conviction they will be liable to imprisonment for a term not exceeding 12 months, or a fine not exceeding the statutory maximum, or both (FLA 1996, s.42A(5)(b)).

Likely sentence

It is not clear how the criminal courts will deal with the new offence. By criminalising breach of a non-molestation order, further sentencing options will be available, including a community sentence. The maximum penalty of five years' imprisonment is equivalent to that which may be imposed by the criminal courts both upon breach of a restraining order under the Protection from Harassment Act 1997, and for some of the more serious offences of violence.

The Court of Appeal Civil Division in *Hale* v. *Tanner* [2000] 2 FLR 879 made clear that there were reasons for distinguishing the statutory provisions for sentencing in criminal proceedings from the approach to be adopted in proceedings for contempt. Current case law in family proceedings, where the courts have been more concerned to secure future compliance than to imprison for contempt, may be of little relevance.

The Sentencing Advisory Panel has already undertaken consultation upon the issue of domestic violence and sentencing (*Sentencing Guidelines on Domestic Violence Cases: Consultation Paper*, Sentencing Advisory Panel (July 2004)). It proposes to submit its advice to the Sentencing Guidelines Council on the issue of sentencing in domestic violence cases in 2005. It is hoped that this issue will be clarified when final guidelines are published, probably in May 2005.

3.3.3 An arrestable offence

Breach of a non-molestation order is now an either way offence, with a maximum penalty of a custodial sentence of five years for persons over 18 (FLA 1996, s.42A(5)). The section 42A offence is, therefore, an arrestable offence under the Police and Criminal Evidence Act 1984, s.24(1)(b). A power of arrest is not required to enable the police to arrest a respondent who has breached the terms of the non-molestation order.

3.3.4 Proceedings under section 42A or for committal

Where a person is convicted of an offence under section 42A, proceedings for contempt of court may not also be brought in relation to the same conduct (FLA 1996, s.42A(3)). Criminal proceedings under section 42A are prohibited where the conduct complained of has already been punished as a contempt of court (FLA 1996, s.42A(4)).

No guidance is offered within the Act as to when it will be most appropriate to opt for the criminal courts and when contempt proceedings are to be preferred.

3.3.5 Range of options for enforcement of a non-molestation order

When a respondent breaches a non-molestation order, several alternative courses of action may now follow:

(a) a criminal prosecution may be instituted under FLA 1996, s.42A;
(b) where the respondent's behaviour upon breach of the non-molestation order constitutes a criminal offence, criminal proceedings may be brought for that offence;
(c) the victim may apply to the civil court to bring proceedings for the respondent's committal to prison for contempt.

In practice, when a respondent breaches an order and is arrested and charged, the respondent may be brought before the magistrates' court the following morning. Therefore the civil remedy may be limited to those situations where the police are not involved or where the CPS decides that criminal prosecution is not appropriate.

Relevance of victim's wishes

If the police have witnessed the breach, they may not need the evidence or cooperation of the victim. Prosecution under section 42A may proceed with or without the victim's agreement.

The government's clear view is that giving the victim alone the power to decide whether to institute criminal proceedings places too heavy a burden on victims, who may be open to undue influence by perpetrators. They suggest, however, that:

> It is, . . . appropriate for the victim's views to be taken into account, and the judge can do so when passing sentence . . . those prosecuting will also take those matters into consideration as would be proper. (Baroness Scotland of Asthal, House of Lords, Hansard, col. 868, 4 March 2004)

3.3.6 Proceedings under section 42A not proceedings under Family Law Act 1996, Part IV

Where reference is made in statute or subordinate legislation to proceedings under Part IV of the FLA 1996, this excludes proceedings for breach of the non-molestation order under section 42A. Section 42A proceedings clearly fall within the jurisdiction of the criminal court. They are to be distinguished from other orders made in family proceedings under FLA 1996 Part IV, including proceedings for committal for breach. The standard of proof in those proceedings will be on the balance of probabilities. Breach of a non-molestation order can only be punished by the criminal courts if the victim's allegations are proved beyond reasonable doubt.

3.3.7 Order unclear or requires amendment

It is unclear what steps will need to be taken by the criminal courts where the defendant argues that the order requires amendment for lack of clarity, or whether the matter will be returned to the civil jurisdiction, which would have had power to amend the order upon enforcement.

3.4 RESIDUAL USE OF POWER OF ARREST

Deletion of section 47(1) and further amendments to FLA 1996, s.47 remove the court's ability to attach a power of arrest to a non-molestation order (Sched. 10, para. 38 to the Act).

The court's ability to attach a power of arrest to an occupation order under FLA 1996, s.47 is retained, to ensure that an arrest can be made immediately upon breach of an occupation order, irrespective of whether a non-molestation order has been made.

In those situations where it remains appropriate for civil enforcement action to be taken in relation to a non-molestation order, for example, if the victim does not wish to involve the police in relation to minor or indeed major breaches, the victim will need to use existing committal provisions and apply for a warrant for the respondent's arrest (FLA 1996, s.47(8) as amended by Sched. 10, para. 38(5) to the Act). If the respondent has breached an occupation order or certain terms of an occupation order to which no power of arrest has been attached, a warrant for arrest will also be required (FLA 1996, s.47(8)).

3.5 UNDERTAKINGS

3.5.1 When undertakings can be made

FLA 1996, s.46(1) permits the court to accept an undertaking from any party to proceedings. The court may not accept an undertaking under FLA 1996, s.47(1) instead of making an occupation order in any case where a power of arrest would otherwise be attached to that order.

FLA 1996, s.46(3A) is introduced (by Sched. 10, para. 37 to the Act) to deal with the situation where an undertaking is offered in place of a non-molestation order, to which a power of arrest can, in any event, no longer be attached. Where the court has been asked to make a non-molestation order, it shall not accept an undertaking instead, in any case where it appears to the court that:

(a) the respondent has used or threatened violence against the applicant or a relevant child; and
(b) for the protection of the applicant or child it is necessary to make a non-molestation order so that any breach may be punishable under FLA 1996, s.42A.

3.5.2 Enforcement of undertakings

Breach of an undertaking will not give rise to a criminal offence. A power of arrest cannot be attached to an undertaking.

It is now made clear that a person who breaches an undertaking may be punished by the court for contempt. FLA 1996, s.46(4) states clearly that an undertaking is enforceable as if the court had made an occupation order or a non-molestation order in terms corresponding to those of the undertaking (FLA 1996, s.46(4) as amended by Sched. 10, para. 37 to the Act).

3.6 EXTENDED DEFINITION OF ASSOCIATED PERSONS

3.6.1 'Associated persons' to include those who have had an intimate personal relationship of significant duration

Section 4 of the Act inserts a new FLA 1996, s.62(3)(ea), to include within the definition of associated persons, those parties who:

> have or have had an intimate personal relationship with each other which is or was of significant duration.

To whom will protection be extended?

This section is intended to offer protection to individuals who have neither married nor lived with their partner, and who are not otherwise 'associated'. This could, for example, include mistresses.

Intimacy and duration both required

It is clear from the explanatory notes to the Bill introduced in the House of Lords (Bill 6–EN para. 31) that the relationship need not be sexual, but should be 'intimate, and personal'.

The government have made clear that 'intimacy and duration are the key elements . . . having determined that there was an intimate personal relationship, the court would go on to decide whether that relationship was of a significant duration'. (Parliamentary Under-Secretary for the Home Department, Paul Goggins, House of Commons, Hansard, col. 55, 22 June 2004).

It will be for the court to determine whether the duration is sufficient in a particular case.

Who is excluded from such protection?

The government's opinion is that short or non-intimate relationships, including short, very intense relationships, long-term platonic friendships and brief sexual encounters such as one-night stands, do not fall within FLA 1996, s.62(3)(ea). Those individuals, if not otherwise associated, must still therefore use the Protection from Harassment Act 1997 (if they can).

3.6.2 First cousins

The definition of 'relative' in FLA 1996, s.63(1)(b) is amended to afford the same protection to first cousins, whether of the full blood, of the half blood or by affinity, as has previously been offered to other family members such as brothers, sisters, uncles, aunts, nieces and nephews.

3.7 COHABITANTS

3.7.1 Definition of cohabitants

FLA 1996, s.62(1) is amended by section 3 of the Act, and now reads:

(a) 'cohabitants' are two persons who, although not married to each other, are living together as husband and wife or (if of the same sex) in an equivalent relationship; and
(b) 'cohabit' and 'former cohabitants' are to be read accordingly. . .

The courts have already made clear that in interpreting the definition of cohabitation, a purposive approach must be adopted (*G v. F (Non-Molestation Order: Jurisdiction)* [2000] Fam. 186).

Practical effect of amendment

The effects of this amendment are:

(a) to open up the availability of occupation orders under FLA 1996 to same-sex cohabitants, whether or not they own the home in which they cohabit, provided they satisfy the requirements of FLA 1996, ss.33, 36 or 38;
(b) to permit same sex couples to apply for the transfer of certain tenancies under FLA 1996, Sched. 7.

3.7.2 Additional considerations for cohabitants or former cohabitants

FLA 1996, s.41, which required a court when considering the nature of the parties' relationship to have regard to the fact that cohabitants had not married, is no longer workable, given the amendment to FLA 1996, s.62(1), and is repealed by section 2(1) of the Act.

The government nonetheless believes 'it is extremely important that the court reviews all the evidence of the relationship between the parties, particularly where the relationship has been of short or sometimes very short duration' (Baroness Scotland, House of Lords, Hansard, col. 860, 4 March 2004).

Accordingly, section 2(2) of the Act amends FLA 1996, s.36(6)(e). Where an application for an occupation order is made by a non-entitled cohabitant, the court must consider 'the nature of the parties' relationship, and in particular the level of commitment involved in it'.

4 COMMON ASSAULT

Key points:

- Common assault is an arrestable offence.
- A verdict of common assault or of other summary offences listed in Criminal Justice Act 1988, s.40(3) may be returned where not expressly charged in an indictment.

4.1 INTRODUCTION

The following amendments are made to ensure that:

(a) the police may arrest a suspect accused of common assault, without warrant, and irrespective of whether an order with power of arrest has been made;
(b) where an offender is charged with but not convicted of an indictable offence, a jury may find them guilty of common assault, where the indictment expressly or implicitly includes an allegation of common assault.

4.2 COMMON ASSAULT TO BE AN ARRESTABLE OFFENCE

4.2.1 Background

Prior to the Act, common assault was not defined as an 'arrestable offence' under the Police and Criminal Evidence Act (PACE) 1984, s.24. The police were often unsure whether they had power to arrest individuals subject to non-molestation orders without warrant. Obtaining an arrest warrant results in delay, whilst the provisions which permit arrest for intent to carry out an arrestable offence (PACE 1984, s.24(7)) and the general arrest provisions (PACE 1984, s.25) are of no use where the alleged offender has left the scene.

4.2.2 Common assault

'Assault' or 'common assault' has been generally used in case law (i.e. *Fagan* v. *Metropolitan Police Commissioner* [1969] 1 QB 439) and statutes (Offences Against the Person Act 1861, ss.38, 42, 47) to include either an assault or a battery. An assault is committed when the accused intentionally or recklessly causes another to apprehend immediate and unlawful violence. A battery is committed when the accused intentionally or recklessly inflicts unlawful force. It is clear from the explanatory notes to the Bill (HL Bill 6–EN para. 47) that the government intend that the term 'common assault' should include assault and/or battery and that it should include a range of actions from threats of violence and striking to unlawful imprisonment.

4.2.3 What the Act does

Section 10(1) of the Act amends PACE 1984, Sched. 1A to include common assault within the list of specific arrestable offences.

In cases of domestic violence

The police now have unequivocal power to arrest in cases of common assault. Their powers enable removal of the alleged perpetrator from the scene of an incident and prevention of their immediate return, even where no order has been made under the FLA 1996 or the Protection from Harassment Act 1997, and where there is no proven threat of further assault. The police also retain their powers under PACE 1984, and have new powers to arrest upon breach of any non-molestation order (see 3.3.3).

Police powers to arrest for common assault of general application

The fact that common assault will be an arrestable offence will also enable the police to arrest offenders in situations of public disorder where assaults have taken place, and where they might have had difficulty in ascertaining whether their general powers of arrest apply.

Citizen's arrest for common assault

Since anyone may arrest an individual who is, or who they have reasonable grounds to believe is, committing an arrestable offence (PACE 1984, s.24(4)), and where an arrestable offence has been committed, to arrest an individual who is guilty or who they have reasonable grounds to suspect is guilty (PACE 1984, s.24(5)), anyone may now arrest someone who has committed or who is in the process of committing common assault.

4.3 COMMON ASSAULT ETC. AS ALTERNATIVE VERDICT

4.3.1 Background

The Criminal Law Act 1967, s.6(3) states that where a person is tried on indictment for any offence except treason or murder and the jury find him not guilty of the offence specifically charged in the indictment, the jury may find him guilty of an alternative offence. The allegations in the indictment must expressly or implicitly amount to, or include, an allegation of the alternative offence. That alternative offence must fall within the jurisdiction of the Crown Court. Criminal Justice Act 1988, s.39 made common assault a summary offence, falling outside the jurisdiction of the Crown Court.

The Criminal Justice Act 1988, s.40(1) allows a specific count of common assault to be included in an indictment if either founded on the same facts or evidence as a count charging an indictable offence, or part of a series of offences of the same or similar character. The facts or evidence relating to the summary offence must have been disclosed to the magistrates' court or be disclosed in certain material served on the accused.

A problem, first highlighted in *R* v. *Mearns* [1991] 1 QB 82, arises where the prosecution fail to include the count of common assault on the indictment, under the Criminal Justice Act 1988, s.40(1). A conviction of the alternative offence of common assault cannot stand.

4.3.2 What the Act does

Section 11 of the Act inserts new Criminal Law Act 1967, s.6(3A) and (3B).

Specified summary offences as an alternative verdict

Section 6(3A) ensures that all those summary offences to which the Criminal Justice Act 1988, s.40 applies now fall within the jurisdiction of the court hearing the allegations in an indictment.

The offences to which the Criminal Justice Act 1988, s.40 apply (CJA 1988, s.40(3)) are:

- common assault;
- assaulting a prison custody officer;
- assaulting a secure training centre custody officer;
- taking and driving away;
- driving while disqualified;
- criminal damage, valued at less than £5,000;
- any summary offence specified under s.40(4), being any summary offence to be specified by order of the Secretary of State, which is punishable with imprisonment or involves obligatory or discretionary disqualification from driving.

Inclusion of all the section 40(3) offences is unlikely to have great impact. Certain offences are unlikely to be alternative to an indictable offence charged on an indictment (for example, driving while disqualified). If not expressly or impliedly included in the unproved allegation, they do need to be included in a specific count.

Power of the Crown Court to deal with such offences

The Criminal Law Act 1967, s.6(3B) confirms that if a person is convicted of an offence by virtue of section 6(3A) of that Act, the Crown Court may only deal with them in the same manner as a magistrates' court could have dealt with him.

The sentencing power of the Crown Court where an alternative verdict has been returned under the Criminal Law Act 1967, s.6(3) is therefore limited to the same extent as under the Criminal Justice Act 1988, s.40. The Crown Court may only sentence the offender to a penalty available on summary conviction. The maximum penalty that can be awarded for common assault under section 6(3B) remains six months' imprisonment, a fine not exceeding level 5 on the standard scale, or both (Criminal Justice Act 1988, s.39).

5 RESTRAINING ORDERS

Key points:

- Restraining orders prohibiting any behaviour specified in the order may be made on conviction for any criminal offence.
- Restraining orders on acquittal possible, on the same terms.
- Victims will be given an opportunity to make representations where the court considers an application for variation or discharge.
- Court may vary or discharge an order upon dealing with the defendant for breach of a restraining order.

5.1 BACKGROUND

Section 5(1) of the Protection from Harassment Act (PHA) 1997 previously permitted a criminal court to make a restraining order only when sentencing or otherwise dealing with a defendant convicted of an offence of harassment (PHA 1997, s.2) or an offence of putting someone in fear of violence (PHA 1997, s.4). The criminal court could not, however, make a restraining order where there was insufficient evidence to convict the defendant, even where sufficient evidence would have been available to make a restraining order if the case had been heard before the civil court. The amendments made by section 12 of the Act, proposed initially in *Safety and Justice: The Government's Proposals on Domestic Violence*, Home Office (July 2003), extend the restrictions imposed by these orders to any convicted defendant and to those who have been acquitted. Concerns raised in responses to *Safety and Justice*, that victims are not kept sufficiently informed during such proceedings, are partially addressed.

5.2 RESTRAINING ORDER AVAILABLE WHERE DEFENDANT CONVICTED OF ANY OFFENCE

By deleting reference to PHA 1997, ss.2 and 4 from PHA 1997, s.5(1), the Act (s.12(1)) empowers the criminal court to make a restraining order ('a section 5 order') as well as sentencing him or dealing with him in any other way, whenever a defendant is convicted of any offence.

5.2.1 No requirement that conviction be for domestic violence or harassment

If a defendant is convicted for breach of a non-molestation order under the Family Law Act (FLA) 1996, s.42A, a section 5 order may be made, whether or not sought by the victim. There is, however, no requirement that the conviction which triggers use of section 5 is for domestic violence or harassment.

5.2.2 Order offers protection 'from conduct'

The previous requirement that the order be made for the purpose of protecting the victim 'from further conduct which amounts to harassment or will cause a fear of violence' is deleted. The order may be made for the purpose of protecting the victim 'from conduct' which amounts to harassment or will cause a fear of violence (PHA 1997, s.5(2), as amended by Sched. 10, para. 43(3)) to the Act.

Whilst there appears to be no explicit requirement to prove that the defendant has previously pursued a course of conduct amounting to harassment, or that he has caused a fear of violence, the government confirms that 'the clear purpose of the order is to prevent future harassment, and a court can make an order only if it is satisfied that it is necessary for that purpose' (Baroness Scotland of Asthal, House of Lords, Hansard, col. GC250, 2 February 2004).

5.3 RESTRAINING ORDERS ON ACQUITTAL

PHA 1997, s.5A, inserted by section 12(5) of the Act, permits a criminal court, of its own volition, to make a restraining order ('a section 5A order') when the defendant is acquitted if it considers it necessary to protect a person from harassment by the defendant.

5.3.1 Related offence need not be an offence of violence or harassment

The wording of PHA 1997, s.5A is broad:

> A court before which a person ('the defendant') is acquitted of an offence may, if it considers it necessary to do so to protect a person from harassment by the defendant, make an order prohibiting the defendant from doing anything described in the order' (PHA 1997, s.5A(1)).

This avoids the need for the court to relate the restraining order to the specific offence of which the defendant has been acquitted. The offence need not be an offence of violence or harassment. It therefore enables a section 5A order to be made, for example, where an offence such as criminal damage is charged, following a campaign of harassment.

The government recognises that the amendment is wide, but believes it necessary to deal with those cases where there has been clear evidence during the proceedings that the victim needs protection, but insufficient evidence to convict (House of Lords, Hansard, col. GC 245, 2 February 2004).

5.3.2 No restraining order to be made against a witness or victim

Whilst there may be evidence in the course of the trial which indicates that the defendant and the victim have both pursued a course of conduct amounting to harassment, the section 5A order may only be made to restrain the defendant, who will have had legal representation during the case and will have had notice that their conduct will be examined in detail. The court retains its power to 'bind over' the defendant, victim or witnesses of its own motion at any time before the conclusion of the criminal proceedings or on acquittal of the defendant where it believes or considers that the person's conduct is such that there might be a breach of the peace in future, whether committed by him or others. If the witness's conduct were such as to constitute an offence then their prosecution would need to be considered.

5.3.3 Which courts may make a section 5A order

PHA 1997, s.5A(1) refers only to 'a court before which a person ("the defendant") is acquitted'. This will include the court of trial. PHA 1997, s.5A(4) and (5) clarify the situation where the defendant is acquitted upon appeal.

If the Court of Appeal acquits a defendant upon appeal, they may remit the case to the Crown Court, to enable the Crown Court to make a section 5A order (PHA 1997, s.5A(3)). An order under PHA 1997, s.5A(1) may be made by either the Crown Court which acquitted the defendant upon appeal against conviction, or the Crown Court to which the case is remitted by the Court of Appeal (PHA 1997, s.5A(4)).

5.3.4 Temporary section 5A orders

Whilst, when a defendant is convicted, bail conditions pending sentencing can restrain the defendant from contacting the victim, upon acquittal bail ends. It is suggested that if it is not possible to give the defendant adequate notice to deal with section 5A proceedings immediately, and if an adjournment is inevitable, a temporary restraining order is possible. The power in the new section 5A is to make an order prohibiting the defendant from doing anything if it is considered necessary to do so.

5.3.5 Appeal against a section 5A order

The defendant has the same right to appeal against a section 5A order as:

(a) to appeal a conviction by the court which made the section 5A order, for the offence in question; or
(b) to appeal a section 5 order (PHA 1997, s.5A(5)).

PHA 1997, s.5A(5)(a) suggests that, whilst these are civil orders, an appeal against an order under PHA 1997, s.5A made by the magistrates' court would go to the Crown Court and an appeal from the Crown Court would go to the Court of Appeal Criminal Division.

5.4 PROVISIONS APPLYING TO BOTH SECTIONS 5 AND 5A

PHA 1997, s.5A(2) confirms that PHA 1997, s.5(3) to (7) apply to proceedings under PHA 1997, s.5A, as they apply upon the defendant's conviction.

5.4.1 Duration of order

The court may make an order to have effect either for a specified period, or to last until further order (PHA 1997, s.5(3)).

5.4.2. Evidential issues

Criminal court may hear evidence admissible in civil proceedings

The criminal court will have heard evidence and may have sufficient before it to found a conviction. The court may have regard to the evidence it heard during the criminal trial in determining whether an injunction is required.

Given the courts' new powers to make restraining orders upon conviction for any offence and upon acquittal, further evidence may also be required where conduct to be prohibited is not necessarily the behaviour for which the person was found guilty, or where the court has not heard evidence or sufficient evidence of harassment during criminal proceedings to judge whether an order is appropriate.

Section 12(2) of the Act inserts a new PHA 1997, s.5(3A), which permits both prosecution and defence to lead such further evidence as would be admissible in civil proceedings for a restraining order under PHA 1997, s.3.

Separate civil proceedings

It is clear that section 5 proceedings are civil proceedings, akin to proceedings under PHA 1997, s.3, and that the civil evidence rules apply. The proceedings under section 5 and section 5A are entirely separate from the criminal proceedings in which the defendant has been convicted. It is less clear whether a defendant's criminal public funding will continue for the purpose of proceedings under sections 5 and 5A.

Standard of proof

The government's own view, as explained by Baroness Scotland, as to whether the civil or criminal standard of proof applies to proceedings under sections 5 and 5A seems somewhat confused:

> The Government's view is that the courts should have the flexibility to decide on the appropriate standard of proof in relation to any past behaviour, before making the forward-looking decision on whether a protective order is necessary in the particular case before them. (House of Lords, Hansard, col. GC 250, 2 February 2004)

> The amount of evidence that one has to produce to satisfy the balance of probabilities will differ in accordance with the gravity of the assertion that one wishes to establish. So it is the ordinary standard – not a new standard, but the ordinary civil standard . . . there are cases where . . . even though the court is making a civil order, it might need to apply a higher version of the civil standard in deciding whether past conduct is proved, depending on the nature and severity of the conduct alleged. (House of Lords, Hansard, col. 1229, 9 March 2004)

5.4.3 Variation or discharge possible in proceedings for breach of original order

PHA 1997, s.5(4) permits the prosecutor, defendant or any other person mentioned in the section 5 or section 5A order to apply to the original court for the order to be varied or discharged.

A new PHA 1997, s.5(7), inserted by section 12(4) of the Act, permits the court to vary or discharge the section 5 order when it deals with a person for the offence of breach of the order. The restraining order can then continue to reflect the risk of harassment by the defendant towards the victim, and will reduce the need for victims to apply for the order to be varied to offer further protection.

5.4.4 Limited entitlement to be heard upon variation or discharge

Section 12(3) of the Act inserts a new PHA 1997, s.5(4A), which entitles any person mentioned in the order, including the defendant and any person protected by the order, to be heard on the hearing of such variation or discharge application.

Rules of Court will be introduced requiring the court to inform anyone mentioned in the restraining order of an application to vary or terminate it, so that they can exercise their right to be heard.

It should also be noted that there is no explicit provision in the Act entitling any person to be heard where an order is varied under the new PHA 1997, s.5(7), nor will the victim, who is not a party to the criminal proceedings, be entitled to make representations as to the term or nature of the order when the court considers initially whether the restraining order is to be made.

It is unclear whether the defendant, or victim, can obtain publicly funded legal representation for the hearing of the variation or discharge application.

5.4.5 Consequences of breach

If the defendant breaches an order under PHA 1997, ss.5 or 5A, without reasonable excuse, they will be guilty of a criminal offence (PHA 1997, s.5(5)).

On conviction on indictment, the defendant may be subject to imprisonment for a term not exceeding five years, or a fine, or both. On summary conviction, the maximum penalty is imprisonment for a term not exceeding six months, or a fine not exceeding the statutory maximum, or both (PHA 1997, s.5(6)).

Whilst the penalty which may be imposed upon breach of the new section 5A restraining order is identical to that which has been imposed under the old section 5, it is unclear whether the Court of Appeal's guidance in *Liddle* [2000] 1 Cr. App. R (S) 131 regarding the approach to sentence for breach of a restraining order will apply. Again, it is hoped that the guidance to be issued by the Sentencing Guidelines Council will assist (see 3.3.2).

5.5 RACIALLY AGGRAVATED HARASSMENT

The Crime and Disorder Act 1998, s.32(7) permitted the court to make a restraining order under PHA 1997, s.5 where a person was convicted of racially aggravated offences equivalent to those offences in PHA 1997, s.2 and s.4. This section is deleted, since section 5 now permits a restraining order to be made upon conviction for any offence (Sched. 10, para. 48 to the Act).

6 DOMESTIC HOMICIDE REVIEWS

Key points:

- Introduction of statutory domestic homicide reviews to learn lessons following the death of individuals aged 16 or older, who have, or appear to have, died as a result of violence, abuse or neglect caused by a relative, partner or household member.
- Police, local authorities, local probation boards, health authorities etc. may be required to establish or participate in such reviews.

6.1 BACKGROUND

Currently, when a child dies and abuse or neglect are known or suspected to have been a factor in the death, Area Child Protection Committees are expected to review the involvement of agencies and professionals with the child and its family, to establish whether lessons can be learned about how the various agencies work together, with a view to planning improvements (*Working Together to Safeguard Children*, TSO (1999) Part 8).

The proposal to establish statutory multi-agency reviews for domestic violence homicides was mooted in *Safety and Justice: The Government's Proposals on Domestic Violence*, Home Office (July 2003), para. 75. Whilst the Metropolitan Police Service has piloted a model for domestic violence murder reviews, which is being adopted in other areas, there is no national provision for establishing reviews where an adult dies (*Findings from the Multi-Agency Domestic Violence Murder Reviews in London*, prepared for the ACPO Homicide Working Group, Metropolitan Police Authority (October 2003)).

6.2 STATUTORY DOMESTIC HOMICIDE REVIEWS

Section 9 of the Act provides statutory authority for the establishment and conduct of 'domestic homicide reviews'.

6.2.1 'Domestic homicide review'

A domestic homicide review is:

> a review of the circumstances in which the death of a person aged 16 or over has, or appears to have, resulted from violence, abuse or neglect by:
>
> (a) a person to whom he was related or with whom he was or had been in an intimate personal relationship, or
> (b) a member of the same household as himself,
>
> held with a view to identifying the lessons to be learnt from the death (s.9(1)).

Overlap with Part 8 reviews following the death of a child

Since Part 8 reviews enable agencies to consider lessons where any child, including those aged 16 or 17, has died, there will be some overlap between Part 8 reviews and domestic homicide reviews. The government makes clear, however, that:

> None of us wants two separate and parallel reviews to take place; nor do we want a review that examines only the domestic violence and not the death of the children, or – as would happen under the current legislation – a review that examined only the death of the children, but could not examine the context of domestic violence in which the children were killed. The legislation and its accompanying guidance will address that. (Solicitor General, Harriet Harman, House of Commons, Hansard, col. 115, 24 June 2004)

6.2.2 Who will establish and conduct the reviews?

Who will participate?

Under section 9(2) of the Act, the Home Secretary may require certain persons or bodies listed in section 9(4) (subject to amendment by order of the Home Secretary under section 9(6)) to establish or participate in a review. Section 9(3) requires those same persons and bodies, who establish or participate in a domestic homicide review, to have regard to non-statutory guidance to be issued by the Home Secretary.

It is inferred from the wording of these subsections, and has been confirmed by the government, that those persons listed in section 9(4) are not the only individuals who may participate in a review. Whilst voluntary sector agencies are not included within section 9(4), because it was not considered appropriate to compel them to act, it will often be appropriate for them to participate in a review. Coroners will only be involved where they have information that has not otherwise materialised and which is relevant to the homicide review.

The Solicitor General, Harriet Harman, clarified that whilst all those invited to a review should participate, others, including friends and colleagues of the deceased who have not been invited, need to be made aware that there is a review and that they can come forward to give their information to the review (House of Commons, Hansard, col. 138, 24 June 2004).

Participation may be required

The Solicitor General, Harriet Harman, also confirmed (House of Commons, Hansard, col. 116–7, 24 June 2004) that the guidance is intended to be wide enough to enable agencies to determine which issues and which parties should be involved in the review, permitting agencies voluntarily to establish a review. Section 9(2) grants the Home Secretary a narrow legislative authority to require reluctant agencies to participate.

The following persons and bodies within England and Wales may be required to establish or participate in a domestic homicide review and must have regard to guidance issued by the Secretary of State as to establishment and conduct of reviews:

- chief officers of police for police areas in England and Wales;
- local authorities, defined by section 9(5) to mean, in relation to England, the council of a district, county or London borough, the Common Council of the City of London and the Council of the Isles of Scilly and in relation to Wales, the council of a county or county borough; this includes local education authorities and social services departments;
- local probation boards established under the Criminal Justice and Court Services Act 2000, s.4;
- strategic health authorities established under the National Health Service Act 1977, s.8;
- Primary Care Trusts established under the National Health Service Act 1977, s.16A;
- local health boards established under the National Health Service Act 1977, s.16BA;
- NHS trusts established under the National Health Service and Community Care Act 1990, s.5 (which definition includes mental health trusts).

Leadership of reviews

Safety and Justice suggested that the police might be a suitable lead agency. However, the Greater London Domestic Violence Project, noting the 1996 report by Gill Hague and Ellen Malos with Wendy Dear, *Multi-Agency Work and Domestic Violence: A National Study of Inter-Agency Initiatives*, Policy Press and Joseph Rowntree Foundation (1996), suggested that police-led initiatives are less effective. The government does not oppose leadership by a voluntary agency (subject to resources) or from the health sector, but has yet to determine whether a specific model or local practices should be adopted.

6.2.3 When must a review be conducted?

The Act does not clarify if a review must take place whenever the circumstances mentioned in section 9(1) arise. A certain amount of discretion will be given to those named in section 9(4) to 'institute such reviews as appear to them proper and consistent with the number of deaths that occur in their area' (Baroness Scotland of Asthal, House of Lords, Hansard, col. GC228, 2 February 2004).

Baroness Scotland did clarify, however, that:

> We intend, as far as possible, to draw on the guidance already used for serious case reviews following child deaths and the guidance used currently by the Metropolitan Police for its domestic violence homicide reviews, which in turn draws heavily on the serious case review guidance. (House of Lords, Hansard, col. GC227, 2 February 2004)

The Guidelines for Multi-Agency Domestic Violence Murder Reviews suggest that a review should always take place when a victim of domestic violence dies, and should be considered where potentially life-threatening injury or serious and permanent impairment of health or development is suffered following abuse or serious sexual assault (*Findings from the Multi-Agency Domestic Violence Murder Reviews in London* App. V).

No criminal conviction needed

The fact that the death 'appears to have resulted from' makes clear that a criminal conviction is not a prerequisite to a review. A review should not be delayed as a matter of course, when there is a pending prosecution or criminal proceedings. Where relevant evidence subsequently arises in a criminal case, such information must be fed back into the review process.

6.2.4 How reviews will be conducted

The non-statutory guidance to be issued by the Home Secretary will 'encourage multi-agency reviews in relevant cases and will provide details as to leadership, format, timing and participants depending on the individual circumstances of the case' (Explanatory notes HL Bill 6–EN para. 43, Bill 83–EN, para. 45).

At present it is not proposed that the reviews be held in public (Solicitor General, Harriet Harman, House of Commons, Hansard, col. 139, 24 June 2004). The Data Protection Act 1998 does allow information to be shared for the purposes of avoidance of crime, yet professional confidentiality remains an issue for some professionals even after death.

PART III **CRIMINAL LAW**

7 OFFENCE OF CAUSING OR ALLOWING DEATH

Key points:

- A new homicide offence introduced, applying to those defendants who cause or allow the death of a child or vulnerable adult.
- Defendant must be a member of the same household as the deceased who has had frequent contact with the deceased.
- A defendant will be guilty where they caused the death or were, or ought to have been, aware that the deceased was at risk and took no reasonable steps to prevent a death which was foreseeable.
- The new offence may be jointly charged with murder or manslaughter and if jointly charged:
  - the submission of no case to answer is postponed until all evidence has been given;
  - the charge of murder or manslaughter may not be dismissed until the charge relating to the new offence has been dismissed;
  - adverse inferences which may be drawn in relation to the new offence may also be drawn in relation to the charge of murder or manslaughter.
- Consideration of how sections 5 and 6 may operate in practice.

7.1 BACKGROUND

Where a child is killed by one of two carers, the trial judge must withdraw a charge of murder or manslaughter from the jury at the conclusion of the prosecution evidence, if the prosecution are unable to establish a case to answer against either defendant (*R* v. *Lane and Lane* (1986) 82 Cr. App. R 5). Where one parent struck the fatal blow, and the other is culpable through active participation in the killing, or by failing to protect the child, neither may be convicted.

The Act introduces a new offence of homicide applying where the deceased was a child or a vulnerable adult. Significant amendments to procedure are introduced, to provoke defendants into providing evidence against each other in cases where the offence is jointly charged with an offence of murder or manslaughter.

7.2 THE OFFENCE

7.2.1 Section 5(1) of the Act

Section 5(1) provides that a defendant is guilty of an offence if:

(a) a child or vulnerable adult dies as a result of the unlawful act of a person who:

  (i) was a member of the same household as the deceased, and
  (ii) had frequent contact with him,

(b) the defendant was a member of the same household who had frequent contact with the deceased, and
(c) at that time there was a significant risk of serious physical harm being caused to the victim by the unlawful act of such a person, and
(d) either the defendant caused the deceased's death or:

  (i) the defendant, who was, or ought to have been, aware of the risk mentioned in paragraph (c),
  (ii) failed to take such steps as he could reasonably have been expected to take to protect the deceased from the risk, and
  (iii) the act occurred in circumstances of the kind that the defendant foresaw or ought to have foreseen.

7.2.2 Victim to be a child or vulnerable adult

A 'child' is a person under the age of 16 (s.5(6)).

A 'vulnerable adult' means a person aged 16 or over whose ability to protect himself from violence, abuse or neglect is significantly impaired through physical or mental disability or illness, through old age or otherwise (s.5(6)).

It does not extend to adults in institutional care.

The words 'or otherwise' within section 5(6) should be construed in the light of the preceding words and are connected to those words. The crucial part of the definition is that the person's 'ability to protect himself from violence, abuse or neglect is significantly impaired'.

7.2.3 Victim's death required

Section 6(5) confirms that this is an offence of homicide, for the purposes of the Magistrates Court Act 1980, ss.24 and 25, Crime and Disorder Act 1998, s.51A and Powers of Criminal Courts (Sentencing) Act 2000, s.8.

Non-accidental serious injury or harm is relevant only to the extent that it may presage the death of the child or vulnerable adult.

7.2.4 Unlawful act required

An unlawful act means an act or an omission that constitutes an offence, or that would constitute an offence if the defendant had not lacked criminal responsibility (s.5(5) and (6)).

The section does not apply in cases of accidental death.

Section 5(5) safeguards the person who lacks criminal responsibility, who may have caused the death, from prosecution, if they could not otherwise have been charged with an offence. It must be noted, however, that a defendant can be charged with failing to take reasonable steps to protect the victim, even where the victim died as a result of the act of a person who lacked criminal responsibility.

7.2.5 Must be member of the same household

'Same household'

Where the deceased lived in different households at different times, 'the same household' means the household where the deceased suffered fatal harm leading to their death (s.5(4)(b)). Members of a second household in which the deceased resided would not be responsible for the actions of those in the first household.

Member of household

Section 5(4)(a) confirms that a person is a 'member' of a household, even if he does not live in that household, if he visits it so often and for such periods of time that it is reasonable to regard him as a member of it. This provision therefore ensures someone, who visits the household frequently and for long periods is 'a member of the household'.

The definition is wide and covers a much wider range of individuals than merely those with opportunity to commit or prevent an unlawful act. Those with no relationship or nexus to the deceased or involvement with the arrangement of the household will be caught. A lodger who lives with a family would be a member of the same household, as would a parent's new partner.

The offence is:

> drafted with the idea that members of the household will know enough about the activities of the other members that they can be expected to be aware of the risk to the victim and take action. They are 'complicit' in the offence, either directly or by proximity, through standing by during the preceding abuse or neglect and doing nothing (Baroness Scotland of Asthal, House of Lords, Hansard, col. GC361, 21 January 2004).

Ad hoc carers and babysitters, or someone who is a member of the blood family who lives away and comes home only occasionally, are unlikely to be members of the household.

7.2.6 Must have had frequent contact with the deceased

The offence is intended to catch those who are most likely to be aware of the risk of harm to the victim and who are in a position to ensure that steps are taken to protect the victim from harm. The government suggests that those with frequent contact with the victim are likely to be in a position to observe the ill-treatment or neglect and any other evidence of the threat to the victim and then to take the reasonable steps that are necessary.

The rationale behind section 5(1)(a)(ii) is that frequent contact and proximity to a child or vulnerable adult in its own home should result in responsibility for that person:

> The key issue is the frequent contact with the victim and the knowledge that the victim is at risk. Such contact might come from being in the same room as the victim on frequent occasions and seeing his bruises, or actually witnessing the abuse. It does not seem necessary for the person, for example, actually to have talked to the victim . . . carried him, fed him or undertaken any form of care. (Baroness Scotland, House of Lords, Hansard, col. 1149, 9 March 2004)

7.2.7 Significant risk of serious physical harm

Section 5(1)(c) requires the deceased to have been at significant risk of serious physical harm from an unlawful act.

Such a risk is likely to be demonstrated by a history of violence towards the vulnerable person or towards others in the household. The offence will not apply if the victim died of a blow when there was no previous history of abuse nor any reason to suspect a risk.

'Serious' harm

'Serious' harm means harm that amounts to grievous bodily harm according to the Offences Against the Person Act 1861 (s.5(6)).

7.2.8 Defendant either to have caused or have allowed the death

No requirement to prove which alternative applies

The prosecution does not have to prove whether it is the first alternative in section 5(1)(d) (that the defendant caused the death) or the second (section 5(1)(d) (i) to (iii)) that applies. Where there are two defendants and it is established that one caused the death, whilst the other failed to take reasonable steps to prevent it, the prosecution does not have to prove which is which.

Since the prosecution is under no obligation to prove which defendant did what, a jury could convict both defendants on the basis that they are sure one or both of them had something to do with the child's death while retaining some doubt over what it specifically is the defendants did or unreasonably failed to do.

It is not necessary for the jury to confirm the basis upon which the defendant has been convicted. Unless an application for a special verdict is returned to ascertain the basis of the jury's verdict, the judge may sentence the defendant on the basis that they killed the child, when the jury did not in fact believe this to be the case.

7.2.9 Objective tests imposed?

Section 5(1)(d)(i) applies to the defendant who was or ought to have been aware of the risk. The government argues that since the offence refers to 'a significant risk of serious physical harm', the signs of that risk would be evident.

Section 5(1)(d)(iii) refers to circumstances that the defendant 'foresaw or ought to have foreseen'.

It would appear that objective tests are imposed.

It seems, however, that the government does expect the court to look at the particular circumstances of the case and specific characteristics of the defendant. The question of whether this is truly an objective test is blurred. The government, for example:

> do not . . . envisage that a member of the household who could not have reasonably foreseen the risk would be caught by this offence. For example, it may be that an elderly grandmother in the household was too confused to recognise and act on any sign of risk . . . It would be difficult to argue that in her circumstances the confused grandmother could have foreseen the risk, must less ought to have done so. (Baroness Scotland, House of Lords, Hansard, col. 1158, 9 March 2004)

7.2.10 'Reasonable steps'

The decision as to what are 'reasonable steps' is for the jury to make, upon direction from the judge.

It is not necessary for the prosecution to show that the defendant was present at the time when the death or serious injury resulting in death took place. It is sufficient that they knew of the risk. The requirement to take reasonable steps could and may be a requirement to take reasonable steps at the time of the death, but the defendant may also have failed to take reasonable steps, such as alerting social services, much earlier.

The fact that the defendant is living in a violent household and may themselves be vulnerable will be relevant in determining whether they have taken reasonable steps. In deciding what is reasonable it will be necessary to look at the nature of the relationship, frequency of contact, what was reasonable in those circumstances, what was the purpose of the intervention, what it was reasonable to do, etc. The government indicates that 'perfection' is not sought (see Baroness Scotland, House of Lords, Hansard, col. GC351 21 January 2004).

7.2.11 Relevance of defendant's age

Only those aged 16 or over can be guilty of the offence, unless they are the mother or father of the victim. Parents of a child are expected to take reasonable steps to protect their child even if they, themselves, are under 16 (s.5(3)(a)).

No duty to take reasonable steps to prevent harm to a sibling or any other vulnerable person in the household is imposed on a child aged under 16 (s.5(3)(b)). Whilst age will be relevant in deciding the reasonable steps that a person could have taken, the effect of section 5(3)(b) is to impose potential liability on a child, who lives in an abusive household, from the date of their 16th birthday.

7.3 PENALTY

A person guilty of an offence under this section is liable on conviction on indictment to imprisonment for a term not exceeding 14 years, or to a fine, or to both (s.5(7)).

The maximum penalty is deliberately lower than the maximum penalty applicable to murder or manslaughter, in order to provide an incentive to the lesser offender to break ranks and give evidence.

7.4 EVIDENCE AND PROCEDURE

7.4.1 Application of provisions concerning evidence and procedure

These provisions apply where the defendant is charged, in the same proceedings in respect of the same death, with an offence under section 5 and an offence of murder or manslaughter (s.6(1)).

7.4.2 Adverse inferences

Section 6(2) of the Act

Where a court or jury is permitted under the Criminal Justice and Public Order Act 1994, s.35(3) to draw such inferences as appear proper from the defendant's failure to give evidence or refusal to answer a question, the court or jury may also draw such inferences in determining whether he is guilty:

(a) of murder or manslaughter;
(b) of any other offence of which he could lawfully be convicted on a charge of murder or manslaughter;

even if there would otherwise be no case for him to answer in relation to that offence (s.6(2)).

Protections afforded to the defendant

By linking the adverse inference that can be drawn to the existing provisions under the Criminal Justice and Public Order 1994 Act, s.35(3), the protection afforded by that Act applies to the defendant.

Furthermore, an inference cannot be drawn unless the silence can only be sensibly attributed to the accused having no answer or none that would stand up to cross-examination:

> If the jury, when considering the evidence in the case as a whole, considers that there are possible reasons for the defendant's silence other than guilt – for example 'love, fear, loyalty, family solidarity' – it would not be proper for the jury to draw an adverse inference of guilt. Indeed, the jury may be directed that it must not do so. (Baroness Scotland, House of Lords, Hansard, col. 192, 2 November 2004)

What is so different?

For the inference provision in section 6 to apply, there must be a case to answer on the section 5 offence, that is to say that the prosecution will have shown evidence that a member of the victim's household, who had frequent contact with the victim, caused the death. It will also have produced evidence showing that the defendant was such a member of the household and evidence to show that the defendant either caused the death of the victim or was aware of a serious risk to the victim and had failed to take reasonable steps to prevent the death:

> The Government suggests that that situation calls so clearly for an explanation that it is fair to draw an adverse inference on both the new offence and an accompanying charge of murder or manslaughter. (Baroness Scotland, House of Lords, Hansard, col. GC156, 28 January 2004)

The government are making one significant change under the Criminal Justice and Public Order Act 1994, s.35 (Baroness Scotland, House of Lords, Hansard, col. 823, 25 March 2004). Adopting the Law Commission's recommendation, the government have rejected the approach adopted by *R* v. *Cowan* [1996] 1 Cr.App.R 1, which required the prosecution to establish a *prima facie* case before any question of the defendant testifying could be raised. It is sufficient for the prosecution to establish a *prima facie* case on the section 5 offence. It will not be necessary for the prosecution additionally to establish a *prima facie* case on the charge of murder or manslaughter, before the jury can draw an inference in relation to the charge of murder or manslaughter.

7.4.3 Time of dismissal of charge of murder or manslaughter

Where counts of murder or manslaughter and counts under section 5 appear on the indictment together, section 6(3) prevents those proceedings on charges of murder or manslaughter being dismissed until such time as the charge under section 5 has been dismissed.

The effect of leaving the murder and manslaughter charge open whilst proceedings relating to the section 5 offence continue is that where the judge and jury have heard evidence in relation to the section 5 offence, on which one or other of the parties properly could be found guilty of the murder, the jury can still find the defendant guilty of murder.

7.4.4 Postponement of submission of 'no case to answer'

The provisions relating to the postponement of submission of no case to answer apply where the prosecution has established a case to answer in relation to the section 5 offence, in relation to the defendant himself. The question of 'case to answer' on a murder or manslaughter charge is then postponed until after the defence has presented its evidence (s.6(4)).

At the end of all the evidence it would still be possible to submit no case to answer and for the offence of murder to be removed, so that the only offence to be tried by the jury would be familial homicide. The submission of no case to answer is postponed, not removed.

It appears likely that a technical procedure may be adopted whereby the defence make their submission of no case to answer on the section 5 offence. When the judge then asks for evidence to be called, if the defence states 'I call no evidence', a submission of no case to answer may then immediately be made on the charge of murder or manslaughter.

If there is no case to answer on the section 5 offence, the trial of both the section 5 offence and the charge of murder or manslaughter ceases.

7.5 PRACTICAL EFFECTS OF SECTIONS 5 AND 6

The drafting of the section 5 offence means that it should be relatively easy for the prosecution to prove a case to answer on that offence. If the prosecution proves a case to answer on the section 5 offence, no submission of case to answer may be made in relation to the charge of murder or manslaughter until the end of the defence evidence. If the defendant fails to give evidence, then inferences may be drawn in relation to both the section 5 offence and the charge of murder or manslaughter. Any evidence heard in the second part of the trial, whether offered by the defendant or another, may be used to establish the defendant's guilt on the charge of murder or manslaughter.

7.5.1 Evidence is offered by the defence

If the defendant gives evidence to demonstrate that they did not cause or allow the death, any submission of no case to answer can be met with the irresistible argument that the state of evidence has changed since the close of the prosecution case. That evidence may bolster a weak prosecution case.

If one or both defendants choose to give evidence, which may be used against the other, there may be clear information upon which the jury can rely in order to find either or both not simply responsible for the section 5 offence but properly culpable of murder.

Alternatively, where both defendants provide evidence that blames the other, the jury considering the charge of murder or manslaughter will have the unenviable task of determining which of the defendants seemed most plausible. There is no *prima facie* case against which the jury can compare the evidence, merely a comparison between two stories, and it is a question of which is to be believed or preferred.

Whilst it might have been presumed that section 5 was to ensure that both defendants received some penalty, sections 5 and 6 together might in fact be considered to be designed as a more subtle tool to find out exactly who committed the murder or manslaughter. If further evidence provided by the less culpable defendant indicates that the other did cause the deceased's death, the government's aim to ensure that someone is convicted of and sentenced for murder or manslaughter (rather than for the section 5 offence attracting the lesser penalty) will have been achieved.

7.5.2 No evidence is offered by the defence

If the defendant chooses not to give evidence, the judge must have express regard not only to the evidence but to such inferences as it would be proper to draw from the defendant's failure to give evidence or refusal to answer a question, when he decides whether to withdraw the case from the jury at the end of the defence case. By the time a defendant who has not given evidence is allowed to make a submission, he will find that the case against him must now include the additional component of a possible inference of guilt.

If a case to answer is proved on the section 5 offence, and the defendant cannot show a sensible reason for his silence, he will probably be convicted of the section 5 offence.

Only if it is apparent that there is no evidence on the murder or manslaughter charge that a plea of no case to answer will be successful in relation to that charge, and that any inference that might be drawn would be insufficient having regard to the matters proved under section 5, will it be advisable to offer no evidence to avoid the greater penalty for murder or manslaughter.

7.5.3 Defendant charged with murder or manslaughter but not section 5 offence

Defendants who are charged only with murder or manslaughter and against whom the prosecution cannot establish a case to answer in its own time will be acquitted at that stage. They would leave the proceedings even if subsequently on giving evidence on section 5 matters, further or other evidence indicated that they may have a level of culpability.

8 TRIAL BY JURY OF SAMPLE COUNTS ONLY

Key points:

- The prosecution may apply for certain counts included in an indictment to be tried without a jury, such application being determined at a preparatory hearing.
- Conditions to be met before the two-stage procedure may apply:
  - number of counts makes trial by jury impracticable;
  - it is in the interests of justice for counts to be tried without a jury;
  - counts may be considered as samples.
- Where a defendant is found guilty by a jury on a 'sample count' linked counts may be tried without a jury.

8.1 BACKGROUND

In *R* v. *Kidd and others* [1998] 1 WLR 604, Lord Bingham LCJ concluded that the practice, in cases of multiple offending, of charging offences as specimens of wider offending was contrary to fundamental principles of sentencing.

Sections 17 to 20 of the Act, adopting one of the Law Commission's three recommendations for redressing the problem of cases of multiple offending (*The Effective Prosecution of Multiple Offending*, Law Commission Report 277 (October 2002)) seek to balance three principles:

1. Defendants should only be sentenced for offences they have admitted or which it has been proved upon trial they committed (see *R* v. *Kidd and others*).
2. Defendants should receive punishment for the totality of their offending.
3. Justice is to be done in respect of each victim.

8.2 SECTIONS 17 TO 20 OF THE ACT

Sections 17 to 20 provide for certain counts to be tried without a jury. Section 20 of the Act authorises Rules of Court to be made for the purposes of implementation of these provisions (s.20(1)). These rules may make provisions regarding time limits and the effect of a section 17(2) order and provide further detail of the application procedure (s.20(2)).

These sections will apply where there are a series of different victims who have suffered from the defendant's repeated similar offending. The facts and evidence, except the date or the name, may be the same. It could apply in some cases of serious fraud, including for example a series of Internet or mortgage frauds, multiple thefts, sexual offences against children or downloading of multiple images of child pornography.

It is not relevant to continuous offences that are tried by sample where there is only one victim.

8.3 PROCEDURE

The prosecution makes an application for the two-stage trial procedure to be invoked. The application is considered by the trial judge, at a preparatory hearing. In the event of a successful application, an indictment is drawn up containing charges chosen to show samples of the offending. A series of linked offences, reflecting the full extent of the alleged offending, is placed in a schedule attached to the indictment.

The first stage of the trial is a conventional jury trial on the sample counts contained in the indictment. The second stage takes place only in the event of a guilty verdict on one or more of the counts tried before the jury. The judge alone decides on the guilt or innocence of the defendant in respect only of offences linked to those upon which the jury has convicted.

8.3.1 Application by the prosecution

The prosecution can apply to the Crown Court for an order that the trial of some, but not all, of the counts included in an indictment are conducted without a jury (s.17(1)). The judge may not make an order of his own volition.

8.3.2 Preparatory hearing

The application made by the prosecution will be determined at a preparatory hearing (s.18(1)), at which decisions about the trial's management will be made. This prevents *ex post facto* application after a trial has taken place on the basis of a limited indictment.

The Criminal Procedure and Investigations Act 1996, s.29 and the Criminal Justice Act 1987, s.7 are amended by section 18(2) and (3) of the Act to permit the Crown Court judge to order a preparatory hearing, before the jury are sworn, where the prosecution have made a section 17 application, either in a complex or lengthy case (s.29 of the 1996 Act) or in a fraud case of seriousness and complexity (s.7 of the 1987 Act).

The defence must be given opportunity, at the preparatory hearing, to make representations against use of the two-stage procedure (s.18(4)) or, for example, to challenge inclusion of counts.

The defendant may appeal to the Court of Appeal against a decision permitting the two-stage procedure, provided leave is granted by the judge or the Court of Appeal (s.18(5)).

8.3.3 Grounds for ordering that counts be tried without a jury

No order may be made under section 17(2), requiring the second part of the trial to proceed without a jury, unless the conditions in section 17(3) to (5) are met:

- section 17(3): the number of counts included in the indictment is likely to mean that a trial by jury involving all of those counts would be impracticable; and
- section 17(4): the counts that would be tried by a jury if the order were made can be regarded as a sample of the counts which would be tried without a jury; and
- section 17(5): it is in the interests of justice for an order to be made.

When it will be 'impracticable' to try all the counts in an indictment

'Impracticable' means that the gross number of counts included in the indictment renders trial by jury on all of them out of the question. It is suggested that where the total number of counts in a case is so great, it will be clear the test is met.

> It is at the judge's discretion whether a trial is impracticable, the first impulse should be jury trial (Solicitor General, Harriet Harman, House of Commons, Hansard, col. 1518, 27 October 2004).

In a case of 200 or more counts, a point will be reached where it is not in anyone's interest to try extra offences which will not increase the sentence. The government's view is that the court should, nonetheless, have the full extent of the offending before it, on the indictment.

When a count can be regarded as a sample of other counts

Section 17(9) states that for the purposes of sections 17 to 20, a count (the 'sample count') may not be regarded as a sample of other counts unless the defendant in respect of each count is the same person.

A 'sample count' is not otherwise defined by the Act. The government suggests its meaning will be clear to those trying cases:

> The reference to the familiar expression 'sample counts' is deliberate – we intended to refer back to the pre-Kidd procedures. Judges know perfectly well what a sample count is. We are confident that the issue can safely be left to the judiciary's discretion. (Solicitor General, Harriet Harman, House of Commons, Hansard, col. 185–6, 29 June 2004)

Rule 9 of the Indictment Rules 1971, SI 1971/1253, which requires charges included in one indictment to be founded on the same facts and form or be part of a series of offences of the same or similar character, will apply. It is intended to apply to repeated instances of the same type of behaviour.

Whilst evidence admissible in relation to sample counts is likely to be admissible in relation to subsidiary counts, and the prosecution can rely on evidence adduced in the part of the trial heard by the jury, it is not necessary for evidence in respect of each subsidiary count to be admissible at the trial of the sample count.

'Interests of justice'

The government indicates that:

> the third condition in relation to the interests of justice is the most important. It is not merely a throw-in line; it includes the public interest and the interests of justice so far as concerns the defendant or defendants. Unless the judge is satisfied as to the interests of justice being fulfilled . . . then that procedure would not be available. (Baroness Scotland of Asthal, House of Lords, Hansard, col. 1393, 11 March 2004)

No guidance has been given in the Act, or during debates on the Bill, as to when the interests of justice will be fulfilled.

Other matters to be taken into consideration

Before making an order under section 17(2), the judge must consider what steps might reasonably be taken to facilitate a trial by jury of all the counts against the defendant (s.17(6)). If the result of taking a step to facilitate a jury trial could lead to the possibility of a diminution in the defendant's sentence, then that step is not to be regarded as reasonable (s.17(7)).

The judge may not make an order that breaches Article 6 of the European Convention on Human Rights.

8.3.4 Order to specify counts to be tried without a jury

The order made under section 17(2), permitting the two-stage procedure to take place, must state which counts are to be tried without a jury (s.17(8)).

It is intended that the judge should also make clear to which sample counts, if there are more than one, those counts, or groups of counts, are related.

8.3.5 The trial

Section 19(1) makes clear that where an order is made under section 17(2), a judge may try subsidiary counts, where the defendant is found guilty on a sample count.

Acquittal by the jury

Sections 17 to 20 do not explicitly consider the position where a defendant is acquitted of sample charges. The government, however, confirms that where the jury acquit, there is no power for the judge to convict on the sample counts (Solicitor General, Harriet Harman, House of Commons, Hansard, col. 1518, 27 October 2004).

Where an accused is acquitted by a jury of a sample count, the presumption should be a direction to the jury to return a verdict of not guilty on the related counts. The Crown may exceptionally request that a count lie on the file, as it already has the power to do so (Baroness Scotland, House of Lords, Hansard, col. GC271, 2 February 2004).

Defendant guilty on certain sample counts only

Where a jury is asked to consider several sample counts, it is possible that they may convict on one or two of those sample counts only. It is suggested by the Attorney-General that where a defendant is convicted of one of six counts, the trial judge might consider it unsafe to conclude that the jury were satisfied this was a repeated offence by the offender. If, in relation to an early period, the jury considered the defendant not guilty, but in relation to later counts were satisfied he was acting dishonestly, the judge might proceed with subsidiary counts relating to that later period (Attorney-General, Lord Goldsmith, House of Lords, Hansard, col. 1399, 11 March 2004).

Role of judge/court on trial without jury

It is envisaged that the same judge who tried the sample counts with a jury would subsequently try the other counts, if they were not accepted, without a jury. The government make clear that they consider it appropriate for the court to take account in the second stage of the trial both the fact that the defendant has been convicted and any evidence adduced in the first stage that is relevant and admissible (Baroness Scotland, House of Lords, Hansard, col. 224, 2 November 2004).

Where the trial of a count is conducted without a jury under section 17(2), the court will have all the powers, authorities and jurisdiction, including the power to make any finding or determine any question, which it would have had if the trial of that count had been conducted with a jury (s.19(2)). The judge is free to come to his own view of the evidence.

8.3.6 Judgments and appeals

In the event of conviction at the end of the second stage, the judge must give a reasoned verdict at, or as soon as reasonably practical after, conviction (s.19(4)(a)).

The defendant has a right of appeal against the judge's verdict or finding, just as they would have done had the verdict or finding been reached by a jury (s.19(3)).

Where the defendant proposes to appeal, they have 28 days from the date of the judgment given at the end of the second stage to give notice of appeal or to apply for leave to appeal (s.19(4)(b) and (5), amending the Criminal Appeal Act 1968, s.18(2)). For the purpose of appeals under the Criminal Appeal Act 1968, s.18(2), time runs from the date of judgment/conviction, not from the date of sentence, if later (s.19(6)).

9 UNFITNESS TO PLEAD AND INSANITY

Key points:

- Issue of unfitness to plead to be determined by a judge.
- Upon finding a defendant unfit to plead or not guilty by reason of insanity, the court may make:
  - a hospital order with or without a restriction order;
  - a supervision order;
  - an absolute discharge.

9.1 BACKGROUND

The Act makes two major amendments to the provisions applying to offenders who are unfit to plead or not guilty by reason of insanity.

9.1.1 Procedure

Section 22 removes the jury's power, to determine issues of fitness to plead, upon arraignment. This amendment responds to the following criticisms made by Lord Justice Auld:

(a) the system of appointing a jury to determine fitness to plead is unnecessary;
(b) most determinations are little more than a formality;
(c) the judge can and does make comparable decisions;
(d) it is cumbersome because it often requires two juries to be empanelled;
(e) it would be better for a defendant to have the issue determined by one jury alone;
(f) it would be in the defendant's interests to receive reasons for any determination.

9.1.2 Disposals

Sections 24 and 25 introduce new powers, which are aligned with current provisions in the Mental Health Act 1983, to dispose of an offender who is unfit to plead or insane, where a jury subsequently determines that he committed the act as charged. The court can no longer make an admission order or a supervision and treatment order. The amendments respond to concerns about admission orders, which permitted the defendant's admission to hospital although the court had not heard medical evidence nor satisfied itself that the defendant was mentally disordered, and which caused problems in practice when the Home Secretary did not issue the required warrant ordering the defendant's admission to hospital within two months. These provisions ensure that a defendant can still receive treatment and support, if appropriate.

9.2 PROCEDURE FOR DETERMINING FITNESS TO PLEAD

The question of fitness is to be tried by the court without a jury (Criminal Procedure (Insanity) Act 1964, s.4(5) as amended by section 22(2) of the Act). A court must not make a determination under that subsection except on the written or oral evidence of two or more registered medical practitioners, at least one of whom is duly approved (s.4(6) as amended by section 22(3) of the Act).

Whilst a judge will now determine fitness to plead, the jury will continue to determine whether the defendant did the act or made the omission charged against him (Criminal Procedure (Insanity) Act 1964, s.4A(1) as amended by section 22(4) of the Act).

Where the question of disability was determined after arraignment of the accused, the subsequent determination that the accused did the act or made the omission, is to be made by the same jury. The jury's right to determine unfitness to plead post-arraignment is therefore preserved (s.4A(5) as amended by section 22(5) of the Act).

9.3 POWERS TO DEAL WITH THOSE UNFIT TO PLEAD OR NOT GUILTY BY REASON OF INSANITY

The Criminal Procedure (Insanity) Act (CP(I)A) 1964, s.5 (substituted by section 24(1) of the Act) provides the court with powers to deal with a defendant where it has been found that he is under a disability and that he did the act or made the omission charged, or where a special verdict is returned that he is not guilty by reason of insanity.

The court may:

(a) make a hospital order under the Mental Health Act (MHA) 1983, s.37 (with or without a restriction order under MHA 1983, s.41); or

(b) make a supervision order under CP(I)A 1964, Sched. 1A; or
(c) discharge the defendant absolutely.

9.3.1 Hospital orders and restriction orders

The hospital order has the same meaning as that given in MHA 1983, s.37 and is made, at the court's discretion, in the same way as hospital orders are currently made under MHA 1983, s.37 where the defendant is convicted of an offence (CP(I)A 1964, s.5(4)).

The requirement that the court make a hospital order, if it wishes to admit the defendant to hospital, ensures that the defendant may only be admitted if there is evidence that the defendant is mentally disordered and that the defendant requires medical treatment.

Obligation to admit defendant

The hospital managers of the hospital specified in a hospital order made under the new CP(I)A 1964, s.5 are obliged to admit a defendant (CP(I)A 1964, s.5A(1)). A court, which is unable to impose a prison sentence on such a defendant, will be able to require a hospital to admit a person found unfit to plead or not guilty by reason of insanity, whereas it has no such power in respect of those convicted of an offence. Since the court itself orders the hospital to admit a defendant, the Home Secretary has no role in deciding whether or not the defendant is admitted to hospital.

Restriction orders

The court retains discretion whether to make a restriction order under MHA 1983, s.41 to accompany a hospital order (CP(I)A 1964, s.5(2)) save where CP(I)A 1964, s.5(3) applies. This ensures that the Home Secretary retains certain powers in relation to the defendant's management in hospital where the defendant poses a risk to the public.

Where the finding of insanity or unfitness to plead is made in relation to an offence for which the sentence is fixed by law (i.e. murder) and the conditions as to mental disorder and treatability are met, the court must make a restricted hospital order (s.5(3)). This reflects current provisions in CP(I)A 1964, s.5(3) and the Criminal Procedure (Insanity and Unfitness to Plead) Act 1991, Sched. 1, para. 2(2).

Defendant subject to a hospital order with restriction subsequently recovers

Where a defendant, having been found unfit to plead, is detained under a hospital order and is also subject to a restriction order, their case may be remitted for trial provided the Secretary of State, following consultation with the responsible medical officer, is satisfied that they can properly be tried (s.5A(4) replicating the Criminal Procedure (Insanity and Unfitness to Plead) Act 1991, Sched. 1, para. 4, which Schedule is repealed by the Act).

On the person's arrival at court or prison the hospital order and the restriction order cease to have effect.

9.3.2 Supervision orders

Section 24(2) of the Act inserts a new CP(I)A 1964, Sched. 1A, which makes provision about the making, revocation and amendment of supervision orders.

A supervision order is 'an order which requires the person in respect of whom it is made ("the supervised person") to be under the supervision of a social worker or an officer of a local probation board ("the supervising officer") for a period specified in the order of not more than two years' (CP(I)A 1964, Sched. 1A, para. 1(1)).

The new supervision order deals with those cases in which the defendant is not mentally disordered but it is still thought that some intervention is required. This new supervision order is similar to the supervision and treatment order previously available under the Criminal Procedure (Insanity and Unfitness to Plead) Act 1991, Sched. 2 (now repealed by the Act). It differs from that previous order in three respects.

CP(I)A 1964, Sched. 1A, para. 4(1) refers to medical treatment to be provided with a view to the improvement of the supervised person's mental condition. The nature of the medical treatment to be provided to the supervised person need not be specified within the order (Sched. 1A, para. 4(3)). The supervision order could arguably require the supervised person to submit for medical treatment for mental and physical illness.

The supervision order may require the supervised person to submit to medical treatment (Sched. 1A, para. 1(2)), but treatment is not a prerequisite to the order.

Arrangements can be made for in-patient treatment, if the supervised person consents, but the order cannot require the supervised person to undergo treatment as an in-patient (Sched. 1A, para. 6).

Grounds for making supervision order

Where the finding is one made on a charge of murder, the court will have to make a restricted hospital order if the conditions as to mental disorder are met. Where they are not, the supervision order is available to provide a structure for whatever treatment is appropriate to address the risk of further harm.

A supervision order must not be made, however, unless the court considers:

(a) having regard to all the circumstances of the case, that the order is the most suitable means of dealing with the defendant, and
(b) that the supervising officer is willing to undertake the supervision, and
(c) that arrangements have been made for the treatment intended in the order (Sched. 1A, para. 2).

9.3.3 Absolute discharge

CP(I)A 1964, s.5A(6)(a) (as inserted by section 24(1) of the Act) confirms that the provisions on absolute and conditional discharge in the Powers of Criminal Courts (Sentencing) Act 2000, s.12(1) will apply where a verdict is given that the defendant is not guilty by reason of insanity or where he is found unfit to plead.

Section 12(1) is to be read as permitting the court to order absolute discharge where:

(a) a defendant is not guilty by reason of insanity, or unfit to plead, and
(b) the court considers, having regard to the circumstances including the nature of the offence and the character of the offender, that it is inexpedient to inflict punishment, an absolute discharge being most suitable in all the circumstances of the case (CP(I)A 1964, s.5A(6)(b)).

9.3.4 Extension of powers to remand for report or treatment

Powers to remand a defendant to hospital for a report on their mental condition under MHA 1983, s.35, or for treatment under MHA 1983, s.36, and to make an interim hospital order under MHA 1983, s.38, have been extended to cover the situation in which a court is considering which disposal to make following a finding of unfitness or insanity (CP(I)A 1964, s.5A(2)). This will be particularly relevant where the court is unsure whether a hospital order is the correct disposal.

9.3.5 Powers of the Court of Appeal

Court of Appeal substitution of finding of insanity or unfitness to plead

When the Court of Appeal substitutes a finding of insanity or unfitness to plead for another finding, it is empowered to make a hospital order with or without a restriction order, a supervision order or an absolute discharge (Criminal Appeal Act 1968, ss.6(2) and 14(2) as amended by section 24(3) of the Act).

The Court of Appeal must make a hospital order with a restriction order if the sentence for the offence to which the appeal relates is fixed by law and the court has power to make a hospital order (Criminal Appeal Act 1968, ss.6(3) and 14(3), as amended by section 24(3) of the Act).

Where the Court of Appeal makes an interim hospital order under the Criminal Appeal Act 1968, ss.6 or 14, the power to renew or terminate that order and to deal with the appellant on its termination is exercisable by the court below, who are deemed to have made that order (Criminal Appeal Act 1968, ss.6(5) and 14(5) as inserted by section 24(3) of the Act).

The provisions permitting remand for report and treatment and making of an interim hospital order, together with the provisions allowing a defendant subject to a hospital order and restriction order to be remitted for trial upon recovery, apply to the Court of Appeal (Criminal Appeal Act 1968, ss.6(4) and 14(4) as inserted by section 24(3) of the Act).

Court of Appeal substitution of verdict of acquittal

The Court of Appeal's power to order the admission of a mentally disordered person to hospital, when it substitutes a verdict of acquittal for an initial verdict of not guilty by reason of insanity, is removed (section 24(4) of the Act repeals Criminal Appeal Act 1968, s.14A).

9.3.6 Defendant's appeal against order made on a finding of insanity or unfitness to plead

A defendant may appeal to the Court of Appeal against a hospital order or a supervision order made under CP(I)A 1964, ss.5 and 5A where leave is granted by the Court of Appeal or the trial judge certifies the case fit for appeal (CP(I)A 1964, s.16A as inserted by section 25 of the Act).

Where an appeal against an interim hospital order is pending, the trial court may still renew or terminate that order or make some other disposal (CP(I)A 1964, s.16B(2) as inserted by section 25 of the Act). Where an appeal has been made in relation to a supervision order, the court below retains the power to revoke the order and (if the court was a magistrates' court) retains the right to amend that order also (CP(I)A 1964, s.16B(4) as inserted by section 25 of the Act).

The Court of Appeal may quash the hospital or supervision order and substitute or amend it as it deems appropriate, provided that the substituted or amended order is one which the trial judge may have made (CP(I)A 1964, s.16B(1) as inserted by section 25 of the Act). Interim hospital orders and supervision orders made by the Court of Appeal under this provision are deemed to be made by the court below. The lower court has the power to revoke and amend supervision orders or to renew and amend an interim hospital order or otherwise deal with the appellant subject to the interim hospital order (CP(I)A 1964, s.16B(3) and (5) as inserted by section 25 of the Act).

10 MAKING OFFENDERS PAY FOR THEIR CRIMES

Key points:

- Introduction of surcharges, payable upon conviction.
- Maximum penalty payable under a penalty notice for disorderly behaviour increased to include surcharge.
- Higher fixed penalties, incorporating surcharges, payable by repeat road traffic offenders.
- Criminal Injuries Compensation Authority (CICA) to be given authority to recover money from offenders:
  - CICA must serve a 'recovery notice';
  - review of recovery determination possible on limited grounds;
  - civil enforcement possible to recover monies not paid.

10.1 INTRODUCTION

In January 2004, the Home Office consulted upon proposals to establish a Home Office-administered Victims' Fund for England and Wales, to fund a range of services for victims of crime from payments recovered from offenders (*Compensation and Support for Victims of Crime*, Home Office (January 2004)). Sections 14, 15, 16 and 57 of the Act implement the proposals:

(a) for the introduction of surcharges to be levied on criminal convictions and penalty notices, and
(b) which permit recovery of compensation paid to victims.

10.2 SURCHARGES

10.2.1 Surcharges payable on conviction

Section 14(1) of the Act inserts new Criminal Justice Act (CJA) 2003, ss.161A and 161B.

Criminal Justice Act 2003, s.161A: court's duty to order payment of surcharge

CJA 2003, s.161A applies when the court is 'dealing with a person for one or more offences' (as further defined by section 161A(4)). It applies when the court makes a criminal conviction. It does not apply when the court discharges someone absolutely, or makes a disposal under the Mental Health Act 1983.

A surcharge can be ordered together with a term of imprisonment.

Determination of surcharge payable

The surcharge to be paid under CJA 2003, s.161A will be specified by order of the Home Secretary (s.161B(1)). That surcharge may vary according to the offence committed, how the offender is otherwise dealt with (including whether they are required to pay any fine) and the age of the offender (s.161B(2)).

The intention is to impose higher surcharges for more serious offences:

> Where a person is convicted of several offences at the same time, we would want the surcharge to be levied on the punishment for the most serious of those offences . . . the level of the surcharge will be dependent on the level of the punishment. (Baroness Scotland of Asthal, House of Lords, Hansard, col. 219, 2 November 2004)

Offender's means relevant

A compensation order under the Powers of Criminal Courts (Sentencing) Act 2000, s.130, takes priority over the surcharge. If the court considers it appropriate to make a compensation order but the offender has insufficient means to pay an additional surcharge, it must reduce the surcharge, if necessary to nil (s.161A(3)).

CJA 2003, s.164(4A) as inserted by section 14(2) of the Act makes clear that the court must not reduce a fine on account of the surcharge, unless the offender has insufficient means to pay both. The surcharge, therefore, takes precedence over a fine but the court is expected to order payment of the surcharge on top of the fine it would otherwise have given.

Exemption from surcharge

Power is given for the Secretary to State to prescribe exemptions from the surcharge (s.161A(2)). The government intends such power to be used if it appears that certain categories of defaulters are being unfairly penalised.

Enforcement

The surcharge will be treated as a fine for the purposes of collection and enforcement (section 14(3) of the Act). Schedules 5 and 6 to the Courts Act 2003 regarding collection and enforcement of fines, and conversion of fines into work, apply to surcharges (s.14(4)). The provisions in the Courts Act 2003 are currently being piloted. Section 14(5) of the Act permits the Home Secretary, taking account of those pilots, to amend the way in which these provisions will apply to the surcharge.

10.2.2 Increase in maximum on-the-spot penalty for disorderly behaviour

Where a person commits one of the penalty offences (offences for disorderly behaviour) under the Criminal Justice and Police Act 2001, s.1, and pays the requisite penalty, they are discharged from liability to be convicted of and sentenced for that offence. The Criminal Justice and Police Act 2001, s.3(2) specifies the maximum penalty that may be prescribed by the Home Secretary for payment under a penalty notice.

Section 15 of the Act, amending the Criminal Justice and Police Act 2001, s.3(2), ensures that the surcharge is taken into account and increases this maximum penalty to:

- one-quarter of the maximum fine for which a person may be liable on summary conviction of the penalty offence, plus
- one-half of the surcharge that could be ordered against a person of the same age, if such person were ordered to pay the maximum fine for the offence.

The Home Secretary, using existing powers in the Criminal Justice and Police Act 2001, s.3(1), subject to the new maximum penalty imposed by section 3(2) (as amended) will increase the maximum penalty payable under a penalty notice and amend the penalty notice to indicate that part of the penalty will go into the Victims' Fund.

10.2.3 Surcharges payable by repeat offenders of road traffic offences

Higher penalties prescribed for certain repeat offenders

The Road Traffic Offenders Act (RTOA) 1988, s.53(1) currently provides for a fixed penalty to be paid by offenders either:

(a) at a level prescribed by the Home Secretary, or
(b) if a lesser sum, that amount equivalent to one-half of the maximum fine to which a person would be liable on summary conviction.

Section 53(3) as inserted by section 16(1) and (2) of the Act permits the Home Secretary to prescribe higher fixed penalties in cases where, in the period of three years ending with the date of the offence in question, the offender was disqualified from driving or had penalty points endorsed on his driving licence.

No surcharge upon first offence

The provisions are only relevant where the repeat offender has, within a three-year period, committed two or more 'endorsable' offences. When the first offence is committed, no surcharge is payable.

Two endorsable offences committed on the same day

Baroness Scotland suggests that the system will give drivers warning that when they commit another endorsable offence within three years they will be liable for the surcharge and that therefore the system is fair (House of Lords, Hansard, col. 205, 2 November 2004). However, if two offences are committed on the same day, no warning will have been given. Upon committing the second offence the driver will automatically be liable to the surcharge.

Subsequent collection of surcharge separate from the fixed penalty possible

RTOA 1988, s.84(2) as inserted by section 16(3) of the Act, authorises the Home Secretary to make regulations permitting the fixed penalty clerk to issue a surcharge notice, requiring a driver to pay an amount equivalent to the surcharge, where:

(a) a conditional offer has been made of a fixed penalty notice under RTOA 1988, s.75; and
(b) a surcharge has not been included within the penalty stated in the conditional offer; and
(c) the driver is subsequently identified as a persistent offender (meaning someone who falls within RTOA 1988, s.53(3)).

Regulations made under RTOA 1988, s.84(2) may provide for collection and enforcement of sums payable under surcharge notices (RTOA 1988, s.84(3) as inserted by section 16(3) of the Act).

10.2.4 Likely sums payable under the surcharge provisions

For fixed penalty notices (including penalty notices for disorder) up to £80, the proposed surcharge level is between £5 and £10. For a fixed penalty notice, (including penalty notices for disorder) which are imposed between £81 and £200 the proposed surcharge is £10. For a fine of up to £1,000, the proposed surcharge is £15. For all community penalties and fines of more than £1000, the proposed surcharge is £30. The surcharge is £30 for a custodial sentence that is suspended. It is also £30 for an immediate custodial sentence (Baroness Scotland of Asthal, House of Lords, Hansard, col. 217–8, 2 November 2004).

10.3 RECOVERY OF CRIMINAL INJURIES COMPENSATION

10.3.1 What the Act does

Section 57 of the Act introduces new Criminal Injuries Compensation (CIC) Act 1995, ss.7A to 7D. These sections will permit the Criminal Injuries Compensation Scheme ('the Scheme') to recover from offenders the compensation paid to victims of criminal injury.

Whilst sections 7A to 7D set out some of the parameters of the arrangements, further detail of the procedures by which the Criminal Injuries Compensation Authority (CICA) will exercise its recovery powers will be set out in regulations to be laid before Parliament and approved by resolution of both Houses (CIC Act 1995, ss.7A(1) and 7D(4)).

10.3.2 Who compensation can be recovered from

Compensation may be recovered from an appropriate person: 'a person who has been convicted of an offence in respect of the criminal injury' (CIC Act 1995, s.7A(1) and (2)). This obviates the need for CICA to establish any liability in the civil courts.

Where a case is going to appeal it is suggested that CICA would wait until the appeal had been heard before commencing recovery from the offender. Where a conviction is overturned some time after conviction, the government expects the money to be repaid. A reduction of sentence, where the conviction still stands, would not affect these provisions (Baroness Scotland, House of Lords, Hansard, col. 268, 2 November 2004).

10.3.3 Amount recoverable

Part recovery possible

Regulations made under CIC Act 1995, s.7A(1) may provide for recovery of the whole, or part, of the compensation paid in respect of criminal injury.

The exact amount recoverable from the appropriate person must be determined by reference to the specific criminal injury, which is directly attributable to the offence or offences for which the offender was convicted (s.7A(3)).

Injuries attributable to alternative cause

It is unclear what liability the appropriate person will have where they have assaulted and inflicted a minor injury upon the victim, but the consequences of that injury were much greater than anticipated because of pre-existing or subsequent injuries.

Recovery from multiple defendants

Where the appropriate person is one of several offenders convicted for an offence, the doctrine of joint and several liability will not apply, since this would permit CICA, in cases where injuries are caused by multiple defendants, to demand full repayment from any one individual, even where the criminal injury is not directly attributable to their particular conviction. The government suggests that:

> much will depend upon the circumstances of the case in question and the facts that are proved or accepted. If the offenders are equally culpable, the CICA will seek to recover an equal share of the compensation from each of them. If one offender seems to be more culpable than the other (or others), the CICA is more likely to make a corresponding adjustment of the apportionment. (Baroness Scotland, House of Lords, Hansard, col. 267, 2 November 2004)

Guidance will need to address whether discretion is granted to CICA to determine who is 'most guilty' or whether CICA will rely on the court's findings.

10.3.4 Recovery procedure

Determination by claims officers

CIC Act 1995, s.7A(4) envisages that those individuals who currently determine claims and make awards of compensation will exercise the sections 7A to 7D powers.

Recovery notice to be served

Where it is determined that an offender is liable to pay compensation, he must be given a 'recovery notice' stating:

(a) the amount he is required to pay (CIC Act 1995, s.7B(1)(a));
(b) the reasons for determining that monies are recoverable from that person (s.7B(2)(a));
(c) the basis on which the amount has been determined (s.7B(2)(b));
(d) the way in which the amount is to be paid (s.7B(2)(c));
(e) the date by which the amount is to be paid (s.7B(2)(c));
(f) the procedure by which payment may be enforced if it is not paid as required by the notice (s.7B(2)(d));
(g) the grounds and procedure by which he may seek a review if he disputes (i) the finding that an amount is recoverable from him, or (ii) the amount determined to be recoverable (s.7B(2)(e)).

CIC Act 1995, s.7B(3) permits this list to be varied by order of the Secretary of State (to be laid before Parliament and approved by both Houses of Parliament) to add or omit requirements or change the description of information sought.

Review of determinations regarding recovery

Regulations under CIC Act 1995, s.7A(1) will permit a review of the decision that monies are recoverable from a person and the amount that is recoverable (s.7C(1)).

CIC Act 1995, s.7C(2) sets out limited grounds on which the appropriate person may seek a review, namely that:

(a) they have not been convicted of an offence to which the injury is directly attributable, for example, another person with the same name is the appropriate person;
(b) the compensation paid was not determined in accordance with the Scheme;
(c) the determination of the recoverable amount determined was not carried out in accordance with the regulations.

Any review must be conducted by someone other than the person who made the original determination (s.7C(3)).

Where a review is undertaken:

(a) the decision that an amount is recoverable may be set aside;
(b) the amount to be paid may be reduced;
(c) the amount to be paid may be increased if 'the interests of justice require the amount to be increased'; or
(d) the original determination may be allowed to stand (ss.7C(4) and 7C(5)).

Recovery proceedings

Where a person does not seek, or unsuccessfully seeks, a review or fails to pay in accordance with a valid recovery notice, the amount recoverable is regarded as a debt due to the Crown (CIC Act 1995, s.7D(1)). CICA is entitled to bring civil proceedings for recovery of the debt.

The appropriate person may defend these recovery proceedings under CIC Act 1995, s.7D(2), on the same grounds as he may seek, or have sought, a review of the recovery determination under section 7C(2).

The offender has no right to question and the court has no power to make findings about the amount payable to the claimant under the Scheme (CIC Act 1995, s.7D(3)), save to the extent that it is necessary under section 7D(2)(b) to consider whether the compensation paid was determined in accordance with the Scheme.

The limitation period applying for the purpose of these proceedings commences either;

(a) on the date when the compensation was paid, or
(b) if later, the earliest date on which the appropriate person was convicted of any offence to which the injury is directly attributable (s.7D(4) and (5)).

10.3.5 No obligation to recover monies

CIC Act 1995, ss.7A to 7D do not oblige CICA to recover compensation. Baroness Scotland suggests that where the offender is unable to pay, or small payments have been made, CICA should consider the commercial viability of making a claim (House of Lords, Hansard, col. 273, 2 November 2004).

10.3.6 Relationship between sections 7A to 7D, claims brought by the victim and compensation orders

Recovery of compensation will not be permitted where compensation has already been repaid in accordance with the Scheme (CIC Act 1995, s.7A(5)). The victim's right to claim damages through the civil courts is preserved, the victim must still account to the Scheme for civil damages recovered (para. 49 of the Criminal Injuries Compensation Scheme). Any monies repaid by the victim, or paid under a compensation order made by the criminal court, would be discounted from the amount to be recovered from the appropriate person.

10.3.6 Recovery under sections 7A to 7D does not affect payment made to victim

The amount to be paid to a victim is not contingent upon recovery of any sum from the perpetrator. Where challenge is made to the amount that has been determined, either on grounds of apportionment or on the basis that the figures are wrong, there will be no re-opening of the question of quantum paid to the victim (Parliamentary Under-Secretary of State for the Home Department, Paul Goggins, House of Commons, Hansard, cols 337, 343, 6 July 2004).

11 ENFORCEMENT

Key points:

- Increased powers granted to authorised officers and approved enforcement agencies executing warrants for arrest, commitment or detention.
- Magistrates' courts authorised to make order requiring disclosure of personal details.
- Proceedings for breach of a community penalty may be heard by different courts.

11.1 INTRODUCTION

Sections 27, 28 and 29 of the Act are intended to improve enforcement and protect the health and safety of those individuals enforcing certain warrants. Whilst similar powers to those provided within section 27 are already available to police officers executing warrants of arrest and commitment under the Police and Criminal Evidence Act 1984, the government does not want the police distracted from other duties to pursue enforcement, unless an offender is deemed high risk and police support is required.

11.2 INCREASED POWERS FOR AUTHORISED OFFICERS

Section 27 of the Act, inserting s.125BA and Sched. 4A into the Magistrates' Court Act (MCA) 1980 confers additional powers on 'authorised officers', meaning:

(a) civilian enforcement officers engaged by the magistrates' courts under MCA 1980, s.125A (this will include fines officers under the Courts Act 2003);
(b) approved enforcement agencies appointed under MCA 1980, s.125B (Sched. 4A, para. 1).

11.2.1 Powers of entry and search

An authorised officer may enter and search any premises for the purpose of executing a warrant of arrest, commitment or detention, issued either in proceedings for or in connection with any criminal offence (MCA 1980, Sched. 4A, para. 2(1)).

Meaning of 'premises'

'Premises' is widely defined by MCA 1980, Sched. 4A, para. 1 to mean any place, including:

(a) any vehicle, vessel, aircraft or hovercraft;
(b) any offshore installation within the meaning of the Mineral Workings (Offshore Installations) Act 1971;
(c) any tent or movable structure.

Where premises consist of two or more separate dwellings, the authorised officer may only enter:

- the dwelling which the authorised officer reasonably believes is occupied by the person sought;
- any common parts used by that dwelling and any other dwelling (Sched. 4A, para. 2(3)).

Limit on powers of entry and search

The power of entry and search may only be exercised if 'reasonably required' to effect execution of the warrant (Sched. 4A, para. 2(2)(a)).

The authorised officer must have 'reasonable grounds for believing that the person whom he is seeking is on the premises' (Sched. 4A, para. 2(2)(b)).

11.2.2 Entry to levy distress

Authorised officers are permitted to enter and search any premises in order to execute a warrant of distress issued under MCA 1980, s.76 where a person has defaulted upon payment of a 'sum adjudged to be paid by a conviction' (Sched. 4A, para. 3(1)). Premises are as defined by MCA 1980, Sched. 4A, para. 1.

Limit on powers of entry to levy distress

This power may be exercised only if 'reasonably required' to effect execution of the warrant of distress (Sched. 4A, para. 3(2)).

11.2.3 Search powers

When may the power be exercised?

MCA 1980, Sched. 4A, para. 4(1) permits an authorised officer to search 'a person . . . arrested in pursuance of a warrant of arrest, commitment or detention issued in proceedings for or in connection with any criminal offence'.

Arrest by the authorised officer is prerequisite to these powers.

Scope of powers

A search may be undertaken where the authorised officer 'has reasonable grounds for believing that the arrested person may present a danger to himself or others' (Sched. 4A, para. 4(2)).

An authorised officer may also search the arrested person for anything which he might use to assist him to escape from lawful custody (Sched. 4A, para. 4(3)), for example, dangerous articles such as hypodermic needles, knives etc. The search power may be exercised under MCA 1980, Sched. 4A, para. 4(3):

(a) if the authorised officer has reasonable grounds for believing that the arrested person may have concealed on him anything which might assist his escape; and
(b) the search powers permit a search only to the extent that it is reasonably required for the purpose of discovering any items that might assist escape.

The authorised officer may not, under either MCA 1980, Sched. 4A, para. 4(2) or (3), require a person to remove any of his clothing in public other than an outer coat, a jacket or gloves. They may search a person's mouth (Sched. 4A, para. 4(5)).

Seizure of items found upon search

An authorised officer who exercises his search powers under MCA 1980, Sched. 4A, para. 4 is entitled to seize and retain anything he finds, provided he has reasonable grounds for believing that the arrested person may use that item to cause physical injury to himself or another or to assist in his escape from lawful custody (Sched. 4A, para 4(6) and (7)).

11.2.4 Use of force by authorised officers

MCA 1980, Sched. 4A, para. 5 makes clear that an authorised officer may use reasonable force, if necessary, in exercising his powers under Sched.4A, paras 2, 3 and 4. Force must be both 'reasonable' and 'necessary'.

11.2.5 Consequences where powers exceeded

If an authorised officer exceeds the limitations imposed on him by the Act, their actions will be unlawful. The legal consequences will depend on the circumstances, but a grievance can be pursued through the Magistrates' Courts Committee, through an Approved Enforcement Agency's own complaints procedures or through legal redress in the criminal or civil courts. It is anticipated that authorised officers will be provided with training related to their new powers, prior to implementation of these provisions.

11.3 DISCLOSURE ORDERS

The Department for Constitutional Affairs is seeking to improve provision of data to courts, including voluntary data-sharing, where necessary to prevent crime or to ensure sentences are upheld (Parliamentary Under-Secretary of State for Constitutional Affairs, Christopher Leslie, House of Commons, Hansard, col. 375, 6 July 2004).

Section 28 of the Act additionally inserts new Magistrates' Courts Act 1980, ss.125CA and 125CB, which authorise magistrates' courts to make disclosure orders.

11.3.1 Meaning of disclosure order

A disclosure order requires the person to whom it is directed to supply the designated officer for the court with the name, date of birth, national insurance number or address(es) of a person subject to a warrant (MCA 1980, s.125CA(3)). It is intended to be used primarily where there is an outstanding fine or community penalty breach warrant against an offender and all other routes whereby they might have been traced have been exhausted.

Information may be sought from organisations in the public and private sectors, including the Crown, but particularly financial institutions and local authorities, which may be of assistance in tracing offenders whose whereabouts are unknown because they have given false information or multiple addresses or have moved address.

11.3.2 Grounds

A disclosure order cannot be made of the court's own volition. An application must be made by an individual who is entitled to execute the warrant (MCA 1980, s.125CA(4)). The order may then only be made if the court is satisfied that it is necessary for the purpose of executing a warrant of arrest, commitment, detention or distress issued by the magistrates' court in connection with the enforcement of a fine or other order imposed or made on conviction (MCA 1980, s.125CA(1) and (2)).

11.3.3 Use and misuse of information

Information supplied to a person named in a disclosure order may only be provided by them to:

(a) the applicant for the order;
(b) any other person entitled to execute the relevant warrant;
(c) any employee of an approved enforcement agency under MCA 1980, s.125B, acting in relation to the particular warrant;
(d) any justices' clerk or other person appointed under the Courts Act 2003, s.2(1) (s.125CB(1)).

A person who intentionally or recklessly discloses information supplied under a disclosure order to anyone other than those individuals within MCA 1980, s.125CB(1) or who uses that information for a purpose other than execution of the relevant warrant, commits an offence (s.125CB(2)). On summary conviction the offender will be liable to a fine not exceeding the statutory maximum, or on conviction on indictment, a fine (s.125CB(4)).

It is a defence to such proceedings to show that information was disclosed, under statute, under order of a court, for the purposes of any proceedings before a court, or that the information has previously been lawfully disclosed to the public (s.125CB(3)).

Disclosure under a disclosure order should not breach the Data Protection Act 1998. The Data Protection Act 1998, s.35 specifically permits disclosure where required by order of a court, or where necessary 'for the purpose of, or in connection with, any legal proceedings (including prospective legal proceedings)'.

11.4 BREACH OF COMMUNITY PENALTY

Section 29 and Sched. 5 to the Act amend the Powers of Criminal Courts (Sentencing) Act 2000 (PCC(S)A) 2000 and the Criminal Justice Act (CJA) 2003, to permit an offender to be brought before a court other than the one originally responsible for overseeing certain community sentences.

The orders in question are:

(a) orders under the PCC(S)A 2000:

    (i) detention and training orders;
    (ii) suspended sentence supervision orders;
    (iii) community orders, curfew orders and exclusion orders;
    (iv) attendance centre orders;

(b) orders under the CJA 2003:

    (i) community orders;
    (ii) suspended sentence orders.

To ensure the new court is fully appraised of the facts of a case where a different court initially considered the matter, the government intends to put in place systems to improve transmission of information from one court to another (House of Commons, Hansard, col. 379, 6 July 2004).

11.4.1 Court to which notice of breach to be given

Where a justice of the peace acting for any petty sessions area receives information indicating that an offender has failed to comply with certain requirements of an order, the justice may issue a summons to attend or a warrant for his arrest (Sched. 5, paras 2(2), 3(2), 4(2), 5(2), 6(2), 7(2) and 8(2) to the Act amending PCC(S)A 2000, ss.104(1), 123(1), Sched. 3, para. 3(1), Sched. 5, para. 1(1) and CJA 2003, Sched. 8, para. 7(2), Sched. 12, para. 6(2).

11.4.2 Court before which an offender to appear or be brought

Detention and training order under the Powers of Criminal Courts (Sentencing) Act 2000

Any summons or warrant may direct the offender to appear or be brought before:

(a) the youth court acting for the petty sessions area where the offender resides, or
(b) if the residence of the offender is unknown, before the youth court acting for the same petty sessions area as the justice who issued the summons or warrant (PCC(S)A 2000, s.104(2) as amended by Sched. 5, para. 2(3) to the Act).

Suspended sentence supervision order under the Powers of Criminal Courts (Sentencing) Act 2000

Any summons or warrant may direct the offender to appear or be brought before:

(a) the magistrates' court acting for the petty sessions area where the offender resides, or
(b) if the residence of the offender is unknown, before a magistrates' court acting for the petty sessions area specified in the suspended sentence supervision order (PCC(S)A 2000, s.123(2) as amended by Sched. 5, para. 3(3) to the Act).

A magistrates' court dealing with offenders subject to a suspended sentence supervision order, where it would not otherwise have power to do so, is also permitted to amend the order (PCC(S)A 2000, s.123(5) as inserted by Sched. 5, para. 3(4) to the Act).

Community order under the Powers of Criminal Courts (Sentencing) Act 2000

Any summons or warrant may direct the offender to appear or be brought before:

(a) the court responsible for a drug treating and testing order or a drug abstinence order;
(b) the Crown Court, provided the order specified that breach would be dealt with by the Crown Court, or
(c) where (a) and (b) do not apply:

  (i) the magistrates' court acting for the petty sessions area where the offender resides, or
  (ii) if it is not known where the offender resides, before a magistrates' court acting for the petty sessions area concerned (PCC(S)A 2000, Sched. 3, para. 3(2) as amended by Sched. 5, para. 4(3) to the Act).

A magistrates' court dealing with offenders subject to community orders, where it would not otherwise have power to do so, is also permitted to amend the order (PCC(S)A 2000, Sched. 3, para. 4(3A) as amended by Sched. 5, para. 4(4) to the Act).

Curfew or exclusion order under the Powers of Criminal Courts (Sentencing) Act 2000

Any summons or warrant may direct the offender to appear or be brought before:

(a) the magistrates' court acting for the petty sessions area where the offender resides, or
(b) if it is not known where the offender resides, before a magistrates' court acting for the petty sessions area concerned (PCC(S)A 2000, Sched. 3, para. 3(2) as amended by Sched. 5, para. 5(3) to the Act).

A magistrates' court dealing with offenders subject to curfew or exclusion orders, where it would not otherwise have power to do so, is also permitted to amend the order (PCC(S)A 2000, Sched. 3, para. 4(4A) as amended by Sched. 5, para. 5(4) to the Act).

Attendance centre order under the Powers of Criminal Courts (Sentencing) Act 2000

Any summons or warrant may direct the offender to appear or be brought before:

(a) the magistrates' court acting for the petty sessions area where the offender resides, or

(b) if the residence of the offender is unknown, before a magistrates' court acting for the petty sessions area in which the attendance centre is situated (PCC(S)A 2000, Sched. 5, para. 1(2) as amended by Sched. 5, para. 6(3) to the Act).

A magistrates' court dealing with offenders subject to attendance centre orders, where it would not otherwise have power to do so, is also permitted to amend the order (PCC(S)A 2000, Sched. 5, para. 2(5A) as amended by Sched. 5, para. 6(4) to the Act).

Community order under the Criminal Justice Act 2003

Any summons or warrant may direct the offender:

(a) in the case of a community order imposing a drug rehabilitation requirement which is subject to review, to appear or be brought before the magistrates' court responsible for the order, or otherwise
(b) to appear or be brought before:
    (i) the magistrates' court acting for the petty sessions area where the offender resides, or
    (ii) if the residence of the offender is unknown, before a magistrates' court acting for the petty sessions area concerned (CJA 2003, Sched. 8, para. 7(3) as amended by Sched. 5, para. 7(3) to the Act).

A magistrates' court dealing with offenders subject to community orders, where it would not otherwise have power to do so, is also permitted to amend the order (CJA 2003, Sched. 8, para. 9(5A) as amended by Sched. 5, para. 7(4) to the Act).

CJA 2003, Sched. 8, para. 27 as amended by Sched. 5, para. 7(5) to the Act states that where a community order is revoked or amended a copy must be provided to the court previously specified in the order.

Suspended sentence order under the Criminal Justice Act 2003

Any summons or warrant may direct the offender:

(a) in the case of a suspended sentence order which is subject to review, to appear or be brought before the court responsible for the order, or otherwise
(b) to appear or be brought before:
    (i) the magistrates' court acting for the petty sessions area where the offender resides, or
    (ii) if the residence of the offender is unknown, before a magistrates' court acting for the petty sessions area concerned (CJA 2003, Sched. 12, para. 6(3) as amended by Sched. 5, para. 8(3) to the Act).

A magistrates' court dealing with offenders subject to suspended sentence orders, where it would not otherwise have power to do so, is also permitted to amend the order (CJA 2003, Sched. 12, para. 8(4A) as amended by Sched. 5, para. 8(4) to the Act).

CJA 2003, Sched. 12, para. 22 as amended by Sched. 5, para. 8(5) to the Act states that where a suspended sentence order is revoked or amended a copy must be provided to the court previously specified in the order.

12 AMENDMENTS TO THE CRIMINAL JUSTICE ACT 2003

Key points:

- Criminal Justice Act 2003, s.58 amended – prosecution appeals may be made in trials without a jury.
- Criminal Justice Act 2003, Sched. 12 amended to align provisions regarding intermittent custody with those for custody plus.

12.1 BACKGROUND

The following amendments to the Criminal Justice Act (CJA) 2003 are introduced to rectify omissions and inconsistencies in that Act.

12.2 PROSECUTION APPEALS

The Criminal Justice Act 2003, s.58 gives the prosecution the right to appeal to the Court of Appeal against termination rulings (those rulings made in a trial on indictment which have the effect of stopping the case). The prosecution may exercise their right of appeal under section 58 only if the judge makes the ruling at an 'applicable time', as defined by CJA 2003, s.58(13).

Part 7 of the CJA 2003 introduced a two-stage procedure for trial on indictment without a jury. The judge invites representations on whether the trial should be tried without a jury, and subsequently the trial is either terminated, proceeds as normal or proceeds without a jury.

> It is intended that the prosecution right of appeal under Part 9 should be available in both stages of a two-stage trial provided that the conditions in Part 9 are met. The amendments will allow for those provisions to be modified in order adequately to deal with the particular diffences that arise in a two stage trial . . . we need to clarify . . . the point up to which the right of appeal is exercisable . . . the existing reference, which is before the start of the judge's summing up to the jury, would not be apt when there are two stages in the trial and the second stage does not include the jury. (Lord Goldsmith, House of Lords, Hansard, col. 1421, 11 March 2004)

The amended definition of 'applicable time' is 'any time before the time when the judge starts his summing-up to the jury' (whether before or after the commencement of the trial) (section 30(1) of the Act).

CJA 2003, s.58(14) as inserted by section 30(2) of the Act, makes clear that the prosecution have a right to appeal a ruling made under Part 7, where the ruling is made at any time before the judge would have started his summing up *had the case been tried with a jury*.

Since section 58(14) explicitly refers to Part 7, and not to all trials without a jury, the 'applicable time' in proceedings under ss.17 to 20 of the Act (Chapter 8) would appear to be any time before the judge's summing up in that part of the trial to be heard by the jury, and the prosecution's right of appeal will not exist in the second part of the new two-part trial.

12.3 INTERMITTENT CUSTODY

CJA 2003, s.183 introduced 'intermittent custody' orders, which allow an offender to serve the custodial element of their sentence over a period of time, but not on consecutive days, before they are released on licence. CJA 2003, s.181 introduced 'custody plus' orders, a term of custody, plus a stringent licence period expressed in weeks.

Section 31 of and Sched. 6 to the Act amend the CJA 2003 in so far as it relates to intermittent custody, making clear that a distinction is to be made between concurrent and consecutive sentences and ensuring that the required custodial period and the date on which offenders will be eligible for home detention curfew purposes is identical for those serving concurrent or consecutive sentences of either intermittent custody or custody plus.

12.3.1 Required custodial days

Schedule 6, para. 3 to the Act amends CJA 2003, s.246(6), which now states that the required custodial days for an intermittent custody prisoner are:

(a) the number of custodial days specified by the court under CJA 2003, s.183 when passing sentence;
(b) in the case of two or more sentences of intermittent custody which are consecutive, the aggregate of the days specified;
(c) in the case of two or more sentences of intermittent custody which are wholly or partly concurrent, the aggregate of the numbers so specified less the number of days that are to be served concurrently.

12.3.2 Concurrent sentences

These amendments clarify that when an offender has been sentenced to wholly or partially concurrent terms of intermittent custody, the required custodial days for home detention curfew purposes is the aggregate of the custodial days less the number of days to be served concurrently. There will be no changes to the release dates on intermittent custody sentences where there is no early release on home detention curfew.

12.3.3 Consecutive sentences

Schedule 6, para. 7 to the Act inserts new Criminal Justice Act 2003, s.264A which applies to:

(a) those sentenced to two or more consecutive terms of imprisonment at the same time;
(b) those sentenced to two or more consecutive terms of imprisonment on different occasions where they have not been released in between those occasions

where an intermittent custody order relates to each term.

The offender will serve a period equal to the aggregate of all the required custodial days for each of the terms of imprisonment (CJA 2003, s.264A(2)). CJA 2003, s.264A(4) and (5) state that on completion of that period, the offender will then be on licence for the longest of the total licence periods. A total licence period is defined 'as a period equal in length to the aggregate of all the licence periods'. The government explains that this means that the offender will 'be on licence for a period equal in length to the longest remaining licence period for any one of his sentences' (Baroness Scotland of Asthal, House of Lords, Hansard, col. 1423, 11 March 2004).

CJA 2003, s.264 no longer applies to intermittent custody (Sched. 6, para. 6 to the Act).

PART IV **VICTIMS AND WITNESSES**

13 VICTIMS' RIGHTS TO MAKE REPRESENTATIONS AND RECEIVE INFORMATION

Key points:

- Sections 35 to 44 align rights of victims of serious sexual or violent offending to receive information and make representations, whether offender is imprisoned or subject to disposal under the Mental Health Act 1983.
- Local probation boards obliged to ascertain victim's wishes.
- Victims may make representations relating to the offender's release.
- Local probation boards to provide information relating to the offender's release.

13.1 INTRODUCTION

The Criminal Justice and Court Services Act 2000, s.69 granted victims of violent or sexual offences rights to be informed about decisions relating to release of offenders subject to certain sentences of imprisonment or detention. It also imposed certain duties upon local probation boards. Sections 35 to 44 of the Act consolidate the provisions of section 69 (now repealed) with new provisions relating to offenders dealt with under the Mental Health Act (MHA) 1983.

A duty is imposed on local probation boards to ascertain whether victims wish to receive information or make representations about certain matters. Duties are imposed on the Home Secretary and the mental health review tribunal taking decisions on the discharge of mentally disordered offenders, to provide information to local probation boards. Local probation boards must pass such information and other appropriate information on to the victim, where requested by the victim, to enable the victim to make representations if they so wish.

13.2 SECTIONS 35 TO 44 OF THE ACT APPLY TO 'SEXUAL OR VIOLENT OFFENCES'

Sections 35 to 44 of the Act apply only where the offence in question is a sexual or violent offence and:

(a) the offender has been convicted of the offence;
(b) they have been found not guilty by reason of insanity; or
(c) where they are under a disability under the Criminal Procedure (Insanity) Act 1964, s.4 but it has been found that they committed the act charged (ss.35(1)), 36(1) and (2), 39(1) and 42(1)).

Section 45(2) defines a sexual or violent offence to include:

(a) murder or one of the violent or sexual offences detailed in the Criminal Justice Act 2003, Sched. 15;
(b) an offence falling within the Sexual Offences Act 2003, Sched. 3 and in respect of which the patient or offender is subject to the notification requirements of the Sexual Offences Act 2003, Part 2;
(c) an offence against a child within the meaning of the Criminal Justice and Court Services Act 2000, Part 2 (as listed in Sched. 4, paras 1, 2 and 3 to that Act).

This includes a wide range of offences including offences under the Offences Against the Person Act 1861; cruelty to children under the Children and Young Persons Act 1933, s.1; offences under the Firearms Act 1968; under the Theft Act 1968, robbery and burglary; offences under the Public Order Act 1986; the offence of putting people in fear of violence under the Protection from Harassment Act 1997, s.4; a wide range of offences under the Sexual Offences Acts 1956, 1967 and 2003 and the Sexual Offences (Amendment) Act 2000; murder, manslaughter, kidnapping and false imprisonment.

13.3 MEANS OF DISPOSAL OF PATIENT OR OFFENDER RELEVANT

Sections 35 to 44 of the Act apply only when:

(a) the offender has been convicted and sentenced to a term of imprisonment for 12 months or more, detention during Her Majesty's pleasure, detention for 12 months or more under the Powers of Criminal Courts (Sentencing) Act 2000, s.91 or a detention and training order for a term of 12 months or more;
(b) the patient is subject to both a hospital order under MHA 1983, s.37(4) and a restriction order under MHA 1983, s.41(1);
(c) the patient is subject to a hospital direction under MHA 1983, s.45A(3)(a) and a limitation direction under MHA 1983, s.45A(3)(b);
(d) the patient is subject to both a transfer direction under MHA 1983, s.47(1) and a restriction direction under MHA 1983, s.49(2).

13.4 DUTIES IMPOSED UPON LOCAL PROBATION BOARDS

13.4.1 Duty to ascertain the victim's wishes

Sections 35(3), 36(4), 39(2) and 42(2) require the local probation board to take all reasonable steps to ascertain whether a person, who appears to the board to be the victim or their representative, wishes:

(a) to make representations about matters relating to conditions, licence conditions and supervision requirements to apply upon release or discharge (ss.35(4), 36(5), 39(3), 42(3));
(b) to receive information about matters relating to conditions, licence conditions and supervision requirements to apply upon release or discharge (ss.35(5), 36(6), 39(4), 42(4)).

13.4.2 Duty to provide information

Sections 35(7), 38(3), 41(3) and 44(3) require the relevant local probation board, when it receives certain information from the Secretary of State or a mental health review tribunal, to take all reasonable steps to provide specified information. This duty applies if the victim expressed a wish to receive information when their wishes were ascertained or, under sections 36 to 44, subsequently does so.

Table 13.1 Specified information to be provided to victim by local probation board

Section of the Act	Information to be provided to victim
Section 35	Licence conditions or supervision requirements applying upon release; details of conditions/requirements concerning contact with the victim/their family other appropriate information
Sections 36–38	Conditions applying upon discharge; details of conditions concerning contact with the victim/their family; if restriction order to end, from when; other appropriate information
Sections 39–41	Conditions applying upon discharge; details of conditions, licence conditions or supervision requirements concerning contact with the victim/their family; if limitation direction to end, from when; licence conditions or supervision requirements upon release; other appropriate information
Sections 42–44	Conditions applying upon discharge; details of conditions concerning contact with the victim and their family; if restriction direction to end, from when; other appropriate information

Limits on information to be provided

The Act prescribes certain information that must be provided by local probation boards to victims. Other information may be provided, at the board's discretion, as appropriate to the case. The extent to which information is shared must balance the needs of the victim to know what is in place and the need to respect the offender/patient's medical confidentiality and right to a chance of successful rehabilitation. It is expected, and indicated by the Act, that information should be limited to what is needed to enable representations to be made and where the victim has expressed a wish to receive information about conditions of discharge, that any conditions relating to contact with the victim or their family may be provided. Victims should not be given details of the offender's address, personal medical information or specific information about an individual's mental health (see House of Lords, Hansard, col. 249–50, 2 November 2004 and House of Commons, Hansard, col. 1449, 27 October 2004).

The Act does not make provision for information provided to the victim to be shared. It is recognised, however, that it would be useful if a victim could disclose the information to Victim Support (Parliamentary Under-Secretary of State for the Home Department, Paul Goggins, House of Commons, Hansard, col. 1449, 27 October 2004).

13.4.3 Duty to forward representations

Sections 35(6), 37(2), 40(2) and 43(2) require the relevant local probation board, where a person who appears to be the victim makes representations about certain matters, to forward those representations to the persons responsible for determining those matters.

Table 13.2 Matters upon which representations may be made to local probation board

Section of the Act	Matters upon which representations may be made (ss.35(4), 37(5), 39(3) and 42(3))
Section 35	Imposition of licence conditions or supervision requirements upon release and what these should be
Sections 36–38	Imposition of conditions upon discharge and what conditions
Sections 39–41	Whether the offender should in event of discharge be subject to conditions and what conditions; imposition of licence conditions or supervision requirements, what these should be; imposition of licence conditions or supervision requirements upon transfer to a prison or other institution and what these should be
Sections 42–44	Imposition of conditions in event of discharge and what conditions

The Act does not specify a time period by which a victim must make representations, but it is suggested that, according to current practice, where victims do not make representations in time for the decision process, it is reasonable to infer that they do not wish to do so.

13.4.4 'Local probation board'

The local probation board required to ascertain a victim's wishes will be the board responsible for the area in which a sentence of imprisonment or detention is imposed (s.35(3)); the area in which the determination is made (s.36(4)); the area in which the hospital direction is given (s.39(2)); or the area where the hospital to which a patient is transferred is situated (s.42(2)).

The local probation board which is required to provide information may not be the same as the local probation board which is required to forward representations. The local probation board in this instance will be either:

(a) the local probation board which is to supervise the offender upon release, or otherwise the board situated in the area where the offender is imprisoned or detained (s.35(6)–(8));
(b) where the patient is subject to a residence condition, the local probation board in the area where the patient is to be discharged, or the board in the area in which the patient is detained in hospital (ss.37(2), 37(8), 38(3));
(c) the local probation board in the area in which the patient is required to reside, the board which is to supervise the offender or the board in the area in which the patient is detained in hospital (ss.40(7), 40(8), 41(3));
(d) the local probation board in the area in which the offender is required to reside or the board in the area in which the patient is detained in hospital (ss.43(7), 43(8), 44(3)).

13.4.5 'All reasonable steps'

A requirement to 'take all reasonable steps' applies to the local probation board which ascertains the victim's wishes and when the local probation board provides information.

This wording is intended to convey a high level of responsibility and to ensure victims are informed whenever they wish it and when it is practicable. This does not require victims to be contacted in writing and information may be conveyed in a meeting or by telephone call (House of Lords, Hansard, col. 246–7, 2 November 2004).

13.5 DUTIES IMPOSED UPON THE HOME SECRETARY AND MENTAL HEALTH REVIEW TRIBUNALS

Duties are imposed upon the Secretary of State and mental health review tribunals where the offender is subject to:

(a) a hospital order and a restriction order; or
(b) a hospital direction and a limitation direction; or
(c) a transfer direction with a restriction direction.

13.5.1 Information to be provided by the Home Secretary

Sections 37(4), 40(4) and 43(4) of the Act require the Home Secretary to inform the local probation board if he is considering:

(a) whether to give a direction lifting restrictions under MHA 1983, s.42(1) (directions lifting restrictions);
(b) whether to discharge the patient absolutely or conditionally under MHA 1983, s42(2);
(c) whether to vary conditions imposed upon a patient who has been discharged.

The Home Secretary is required to inform the local probation board if:

(a) the patient is to be discharged absolutely or conditionally and if subject to conditions, what those conditions are;
(b) conditions imposed upon a patient who has been discharged are varied;
(c) if a discharged patient has been recalled to hospital under MHA 1983, s42(3);
(d) a restriction order, limitation direction or a restriction direction is to cease to have effect, and from what date (ss.38(4), 41(4), 44(4)).

Where an application is made to the mental health review tribunal by the patient under MHA 1983, ss.69, 70 or 75 or the Secretary of State refers the patient's case to a mental health review tribunal under MHA 1983, s.71, the Secretary of State must also inform the local probation board when:

(a) conditions imposed upon a patient who has been discharged are varied;
(b) a discharged patient has been recalled to hospital under MHA 1983, s.42(3);
(c) a restriction order, limitation direction or a restriction direction is to cease to have effect, and from what date (ss.38(4), 42(4) and 44(4)).

13.5.2 Information to be provided by the mental health review tribunal

The mental health review tribunal is obliged to inform the local probation board when an application has been made by the patient under MHA 1983, ss.60, 70 or 75 or the Secretary of State has referred the patient's case to the tribunal under MHA 1983, s.71 (ss.37(5), 40(5) and 43(5)).

The tribunal must also inform the local probation board:

(a) if the patient is to be discharged, absolutely or conditionally and, if subject to conditions, what those conditions are;
(b) if the patient has been discharged conditionally, of any variations made by the tribunal to the conditions;
(c) if the restriction order, limitation direction or restriction direction is to cease effect as a result of action taken by the tribunal, and from when (ss.38(6), 41(6) and 44(6)).

13.6 EFFECT OF TERMINATION OF RESTRICTION ORDER, LIMITATION DIRECTION OR RESTRICTION DIRECTION

13.6.1 Local probation boards

Where the patient to whom sections 35 to 44 of the Act applies is subject to a restriction order, limitation direction or restriction direction and such order or direction ceases to have effect, the local probation board's duty to forward representations ends. In the same circumstances, the local probation board's duties to provide information to the victim cease (save where the offender was subject to a limitation direction, in which case the local probation board retains a duty to provide information regarding licence conditions and supervision requirements) (ss.37(3), 38(8), 40(3), 41(8), 43(3) and 44(8)).

13.6.2 Home Secretary and mental health review tribunals

Where the patient to whom sections 35 to 44 of the Act applies is subject to a restriction order, limitation direction or restriction direction and such order or direction ceases to have effect, the duties imposed upon the Home Secretary and the mental health review tribunals by sections 38, 41 and 44 cease.

14 ADDITIONAL SUPPORT FOR VICTIMS AND WITNESSES

Key points:

- Introduction of a statutory Code of Practice for victims.
- Parliamentary Commissioner empowered to investigate breach of duties imposed by the Victims' Code and by sections 35 to 44 of the Act.
- Commissioner for Victims and Witnesses appointed.
- Home Secretary required to consult new statutory Victims' Advisory Panel on matters concerning victims and witnesses of criminal offending or anti-social behaviour.
- Provision made for disclosure of information to individuals subject to the Victims' Code etc.

14.1 INTRODUCTION

On 27 February 2001, the government consulted upon a revised Victims' Charter, proposals to place victims' rights on a statutory basis, introduction of a Victims' Ombudsman, a Victims' Fund and further measures to support victims of crime (*A Review of the Victims' Charter*, Home Office Communications Directorate (February 2001). The government subsequently published *A New Deal for Victims and Witnesses: National Strategy to Deliver Improved Services*, Home Office (July 2003) promising to implement a number of measures, which are now incorporated within sections 32 to 56 of the Act.

14.2 CODE OF PRACTICE FOR VICTIMS AND WITNESSES

Section 32(1) of the Act introduces a statutory Code of Practice, which will replace the non-statutory Victims' Charter. It sets minimum standards for the provision of services to victims of criminal conduct throughout England and Wales.

The Code, to be drafted by the Home Secretary, Attorney-General and Lord Chancellor, must be published for consultation and laid before Parliament (s.33). The Home Office, in consultation with the criminal justice agencies and victims' groups, produced a preliminary illustrative draft Code of Practice in 2003. Formal consultation upon the draft Code will commence early in 2005.

14.2.1 Service providers

Section 32(1) and (2)(c) of the Act state that the Code will require specific persons with 'functions relating to victims of criminal conduct, or any aspect of the criminal justice system' to provide services.

The draft Code, section 3, requires Victim Support, together with the criminal justice agencies (the Court Service, the Criminal Cases Review Commission, the Criminal Injuries Compensation Authority, the Crown Prosecution Service, the police, the Parole Board, the prison service, local probation boards and youth offending teams) to provide services.

The government does not rule out inclusion of other voluntary or government organisations or the health service, but would not compel voluntary agencies to comply with the Code without their consent (Baroness Scotland of Asthal, House of Lords, Hansard, col. GC411, 5 February 2004).

Since the Code may not require anyone acting in a judicial capacity or who exercises a discretion in the course of functions as a member of the Crown Prosecution Service to provide services, what provision will be made for victims by the Court Service and the Crown Prosecution Service? (s.32(5)).

14.2.2 Recipients of services

Victims and others

The Code will apply to victims of criminal conduct (s.32(1)). Services may also be provided to other individuals, including parents, instead of or in addition to the victim (s.32(3)).

Criminal conduct required

The draft Code, section 4.8, indicates that if conduct does not constitute a criminal offence, the service provider is not required to provide services under the Code.

In determining whether a person is a victim of criminal conduct, it is immaterial that no person has been charged with or convicted of an offence (s.32(6)).

The draft Code states that it is immaterial that the service provider does not believe the allegation or that a person has been charged with a different offence in respect of the criminal conduct (draft Code, section 4.7). The government suggests that 'whether the code should apply in a particular case will . . . depend on a judgment, usually by a police officer, on the conduct which has been reported or about which a complaint has been made' (Baroness Scotland, House of Lords, Hansard, col. GC425, 5 February 2004).

Different provisions for different situations

Section 32(2) of the Act permits provision of services to be limited to:

(a) specific groups of victims;
(b) victims of particular offences; or
(c) conduct to be specified in the Code.

Section 32(4) permits different provision to be made for different victims, different areas and different service providers.

The government expects services to be delivered of equivalent standards, allowing for regional variations, whilst recognising that different sorts of victims have different, potentially greater needs. The draft Code accordingly limits provision, for example, to victims of certain types of criminal conduct and those who are vulnerable. It excludes victims of road traffic accidents.

Under the current indicative draft, the offence must committed in England or Wales. The service provider must be in England and Wales.

14.2.3 Services to be provided

The Act is silent as to the services to be provided under the Code. The draft Code outlines more detailed obligations, focusing on issues such as information, advice, protection and support. Specific obligations of certain service providers, including the Parole Board, have yet to be concluded.

14.2.4 Breach of the Code

The Code will be 'a benchmark against which service provision by statutory organisations can be judged . . . The code would raise the standard of the services that the victim should receive . . . We really want the code to set, at the very least, minimum consistent standards of service that victims can expect to receive wherever they live' (Baroness Scotland, House of Lords, Hansard, col. GC411, 425, 5 February 2004).

The Code is admissible in evidence in criminal or civil proceedings and a court may take into account a failure to comply with the Code in determining a question in proceedings (s.34(2)), for example, if a victim brought a claim under the Human Rights Act 1998 or the Data Protection Act 1998 against one of the public authorities which were subject to the Code. The Code does not, however, give rise to rights enforceable in civil or criminal proceedings (s.34(1)).

If a victim considers that the Code has been breached, the draft Code suggests that a complaint be made initially to the service provider. Where a satisfactory response is not received, the complaint should be taken to the Parliamentary Ombudsman, whose job it will be to enforce the Code.

14.3 PARLIAMENTARY COMMISSIONER

14.3.1 Extended powers to investigate breach of certain duties

Section 47 of and Sched. 7 to the Act amend the Parliamentary Commissioner Act (PCA) 1967, ss.5, 7, 8, 10 and 12. The Parliamentary Commissioner (the Ombudsman) has existing powers to investigate injustice suffered through maladministration (under PCA 1967, s.5(1)). These are supplemented by PCA 1967, s.5(1A) to (1C), which permit the Ombudsman to investigate breach of duties imposed by:

(a) the Victims' Code;
(b) sections 35 to 44 of the Act.

14.3.2 Conduct of investigation

An investigation under PCA 1967, s.5(1A) to (1C) may commence only where a written complaint duly made to a member of the House of Commons by a member of the public is referred to the Ombudsman, who is asked to conduct an investigation. The complainant must consent to their complaint being passed to the Ombudsman.

Whilst complaints of maladministration are made against government departments and authorities, PCA 1967, s.5(1A) makes clear that the complaint brought under the new sub-sections may be made against 'a person'. PCA 1967, s.7(1A) permits the specific individual who is alleged to have breached the 'relevant duty' to comment on any allegations made in the complaint.

Under PCA 1967, s.8(1A) and (2), the Ombudsman may, when investigating a section 5(1A) claim:

(a) require any person whom he believes able to do so to provide relevant information or documents;
(b) compel their attendance for examination, and production of documents; no Crown privilege attaches to any documents or evidence.

14.3.3 Matters excluded from investigation

PCA 1967, s.5(4A) prevents any investigation under section 5(1A) either in respect of action taken by or with the authority of the Secretary of State for the purposes of protecting the security of the state, or regarding the matters described in PCA 1967, Sched. 3, paras 1 to 4 and 6A to 11. The Ombudsman may, when undertaking an investigation under section 5(1A), but not when investigating maladministration, consider complaints relating to criminal investigations and proceedings. He may not, however, investigate action taken by administrative staff of a court or tribunal where such action is taken at the direction or on the authority of any person acting in a judicial capacity, nor may he investigate certain actions taken under the Criminal Injuries Compensation Act 1995.

14.3.4 Effect of investigation

Where an investigation is undertaken, a report upon the finding of his investigations must be sent to the Member of Parliament who referred the complaint and to the person to whom the complaint relates. The report will specify what the person who breached their duty should do to remedy the situation (PCA 1967, s.10(1) and (2A)).

Conduct of an investigation by the Ombudsman does not prevent the person being investigated, or the authority or department by whom they are employed, taking further action in respect of the matters subject to complaint, for example, to remedy their breach (PCA 1967, s.7(4)).

Where the Ombudsman finds that:

(a) the person has failed to perform the relevant duty; and
(b) the failure has not been, or will not be, remedied

the Ombudsman may lay before each House of Parliament, a special report upon the case (PCA 1967, s.10(3A)). He will also lay an annual report before each House of Parliament (s.10(4)).

The Ombudsman cannot enforce compliance with any recommendation. The government envisages 'that the recommendations of the Commissioner for Victims and Witnesses and the report of the Parliamentary Commissioner will be taken seriously by the Government and the criminal justice agencies' but considers it important 'for Ministers and independent statutory authorities to have the right to choose not to accept a particular recommendation because of the wider implications which the commissioner may not have taken into account' (Baroness Scotland, House of Lords, Hansard, col. GC434, 5 February 2004).

14.4 COMMISSIONER FOR VICTIMS AND WITNESSES

14.4.1 Appointment of the Commissioner and Deputy Commissioner

Section 48(1) of the Act requires the Home Secretary, in consultation with the Attorney-General and the Lord Chancellor, to appoint a Commissioner for Victims and Witnesses.

The Commissioner, as a sole corporation, will be able to bring proceedings, employ staff and own property and is entirely independent of government. The Deputy Commissioner will act as Commissioner in the absence of the

Commissioner or if the Commissioner's post falls vacant (Sched. 8, para. 1(3) to the Act). Schedule 8 details provisions for appointment to and tenure of both offices, provision for laying of accounts and requirements for submission of an annual plan and report.

Table 14.1 Authorities currently within Commissioner's remit: s.53, Sched. 9 (subject to amendment by the Home Secretary under s.53(4))

Government Departments (all of which are responsible for or oversee direct service provision to the public)	Department for Constitutional Affairs Department for Education and Skills Department of Health Department of Trade and Industry Department for Transport Department for Work and Pensions Foreign and Commonwealth Office Home Office Office of the Deputy Prime Minister ('The Office of the Deputy Prime Minister is intended to cover local authorities' Paul Goggins, House of Commons, Hansard, col. 269, 1 July 2004)
Customs and Excise	Commissioners of Customs and Excise
Police forces etc.	A police force for a police area in England and Wales Serious Fraud Office National Crime Intelligence Service National Crime Squad British Transport Police (reference is made to the force of constables appointed under British Transport Commission Act 1949, s.53 but the Railways and Transport Safety Act 2003 makes clear that a reference (whether or not as the 'British Transport Police Force') to constables appointed under British Transport Commission Act 1949, s.53 shall be treated as a reference to the British Transport Police Force established by Railways and Transport Safety Act 2003, Part 3 Ministry of Defence Police
Criminal injuries compensation	Criminal Injuries Compensation Appeals Panel Criminal Injuries Compensation Authority
Health and safety	Health and Safety Commission Health and Safety Executive
Legal services	Legal Services Commission
Court administration	Persons exercising functions relating to the carrying on of the business of a court
Criminal justice system	Criminal Cases Review Commission Crown Prosecution Service A local probation board established under Criminal Justice and Court Services Act 2003, s.4 Parole Board Prison Service Youth Justice Board for England and Wales A youth offending team established under Crime and Disorder Act 1998, s.39
Maritime and coastguards	Maritime and Coastguard Agency

14.4.2 Authorities within the Commissioner's remit

It is not intended that the Commissioner will focus solely on the criminal justice system. Health provision, housing and immigration may all fall within his remit.

14.4.3 Commissioner's duties and powers

The Commissioner has three primary, broad responsibilities (s.49(1)):

(a) promoting the interests of victims and witnesses;
(b) taking appropriate steps to encourage good practice in the treatment of victims and witnesses;
(c) review of the operation of the Victims' Code.

'Victims and witnesses'

Victims include victims of criminal offences and of anti-social behaviour (s.52(2)).

Section 52(8)(a) of the Act defines anti-social behaviour as 'behaviour by a person which causes or is likely to cause harassment, alarm or distress to one or more persons not of the same household as the person'. A person is victim of anti-social behaviour if they have suffered from the behaviour of someone who does not live in their household and which 'has caused him harassment, alarm or distress' (s.52(8)(b)).

Where the victim complains that they have been the victim of a criminal offence, they are not required to have reported the crime (s.52(3)(a)) nor is it necessary for anyone to have been charged with or convicted of the alleged offence (s.52(3)(b)).

A witness is widely defined (s.52(4), (6) and (7)). It is not necessary for a witness to have come forward to give evidence. A witness does not, however, include anyone who is subject to, or might be, or could have been subject to criminal proceedings or proceedings for anti-social behaviour.

Specific powers

The Commissioner is granted power under section 49(2) of the Act to:

(a) make proposals to the Secretary of State for amending the Victims' Code (at the request of the Home Secretary or on his own initiative); the Home Secretary is not required to consult the Commissioner nor involve him in the revision process, however, the government made clear in Standing Committee (House of Commons, Hansard, col. 232, 29 June 2004) that the Commissioner will be consulted upon revision, together with the Parliamentary Commissioner and the agencies subject to the Code;

(b) provide a report to the Secretary of State, which will be copied to the Attorney-General and the Lord Chancellor, laid before Parliament and published (s.26(3));
(c) make recommendations to authorities within his remit; he cannot direct action or enforce action upon his recommendations;
(d) undertake or arrange for or support (financially or otherwise) the carrying out of research;
(e) consult any person he thinks appropriate.

The Commissioner is also required to advise any Minister, including the Treasury, upon their request, as regards any matter raised by them relating to victims or witnesses (s.50(1)). Upon request, he must also provide advice to any authority under his remit as to the information that authority provides or should provide to victims or witnesses (s.50(2)). Whilst the Commissioner can make recommendations only to authorities within its remit, it can offer advice to a wider group.

14.4.4 Limits on the Commissioner's powers

The functions any authority exercises outside England and Wales are not ordinarily subject to the Commissioner's jurisdiction (s.53(2)). The Commissioner will principally consider victims of crime in England and Wales. However, the Foreign and Commonwealth Office is also within the Commissioner's remit (s.53(3)) and it has always been the government's intention that he will be able to investigate some issues relating to persons victimised abroad (Baroness Scotland, House of Lords, Hansard, col. GC442, 5 February 2004).

Section 51 of the Act also confirms that the Commissioner, whose focus is services rather than individuals, cannot exercise his functions in relation to a particular victim or witness, to bring or conduct proceedings or in connection with actions of any person acting in or under the authority of those acting in a judicial capacity.

14.5 VICTIMS' ADVISORY PANEL

14.5.1 Constitution

Section 55 of the Act obliges the government to appoint a statutory Victims' Advisory Panel and, to a limited extent, explains the operation of that Panel. In order to ensure flexibility of membership, section 55(2) merely requires the Home Secretary to consult the Attorney-General and Lord Chancellor before making appointments to or removals from the Panel.

In March 2003, a non-statutory non-departmental public body, the Victims' Advisory Panel, was recruited. Section 55(7) states that the current non-statutory Victims' Advisory Panel is to be treated as having been established in accordance with section 55.

Membership of the statutory Panel will initially be identical to the current non-statutory Panel, which comprises:

- 10 volunteer lay members, appointed initially for three years, who have experienced victimisation themselves or are close relatives of those who have been killed;
- three co-opted members appointed to represent wider victims' interests;
- representatives of voluntary organisations which provide services for victims and witnesses;
- senior representatives of the criminal justice agencies;
- a Ministerial Chair from the Department for Criminal Justice, a Minister from the Department for Constitutional Affairs and the Solicitor General.

(Baroness Scotland, House of Lords, Hansard, col. 20, 15 March 2004)

14.5.2 Functions

The Home Secretary is required to consult the Victims' Advisory Panel on matters which appear to relate to victims and witnesses of criminal offences or anti-social behaviour (s.55(3)). The time and the manner of the consultation is at the Home Secretary's discretion. However, it is clear, 'if a matter arises relating to victims that is of some significance, he must consult them' (Baroness Scotland, House of Lords, Hansard, col. GC446, 5 February 2004).

Section 55(8) of the Act confirms that consultation prior to implementation of this section will be treated as having taken place under section 55(3).

A report must be prepared for each 12-month period in which the Panel is consulted, summarising steps taken in response to the consultation and reporting such other matters as it considers appropriate (s.55(5)). The Secretary of State must then arrange for the report to be published and laid before Parliament (s.55(6)).

The Act is otherwise silent as to the Panel's functions or objectives and does not prescribe how often the Panel must meet.

14.6 DISCLOSURE OF INFORMATION

If provisions relating to victims and witnesses are to be effective, information will need to be shared by various bodies. The draft Code includes specific provisions detailing what information is to be shared about a victim and when. However, where information about a victim or offender is shared without their consent this may breach the Data Protection Act 1998 and the European Convention on Human Rights.

14.6.1 Power to disclose information

Section 54(1) of the Act permits disclosure to 'relevant authorities' for specified purposes.

'Relevant authorities' includes:

- a person required to do anything under the Victims' Code;
- a local probation board;
- the Commissioner for Victims and Witnesses;
- an authority within the Commissioner's remit (s.54(3)).

The current list of relevant authorities may be extended to permit disclosure of information to further authorities 'appearing to . . . exercise functions of a public nature' (s.54(4)).

Disclosure is permitted for the following purposes only:

(a) compliance with the Victims' Code;
(b) compliance with sections 35 to 44 of the Act (see 13.1);
(c) the carrying out of the functions of the Commissioner (s.54(2)).

This list of 'purposes' may also be extended to include additional purposes that appear 'to be connected with the assistance of victims, witnesses or other persons affected by offences' (s.54(4)). A person is not affected by an offence if they are the person accused of or convicted of the offence (s.54(5)).

14.6.2 Data Protection Act 1998

Section 54 of the Act does not override the Data Protection Act 1998 (s.54(7)).

The government, whilst confident that the current version of the Victims' Code satisfies the Data Protection Act 1998 (Baroness Scotland, House of Lords, Hansard, col. GC444, 5 February 2004) and intending that any future revisions of the Code will comply with the Data Protection Act, opposed the grant of greater protection to service providers acting under the Code than to other bodies:

> The fact that information is disclosed under the code will often be sufficient to ensure compliance with the Data Protection Act. However in some cases – most notably those involving sensitive personal information – it will be necessary to ensure that other information and other requirements of the Data Protection Act are satisfied . . . If there were a conflict between the requirements of the code and the requirements of the Data Protection Act, the Data Protection Act would prevail. The sanction for breach of the code is investigation by the Parliamentary Commissioner. We would expect the Parliamentary Commissioner to take into account the fact that the code had not been complied with because compliance with the code would involve breach of the Data Protection Act. (Baroness Scotland, House of Lords, Hansard, col. 14–15, 15 March 2004)

14.6.3 Human Rights Act 1998

Whilst section 54 of the Act makes no reference to the Human Rights Act 1998, the explanatory notes to the Bill confirmed that it is implicit that the Human Rights Act 1998 must be taken into account before any disclosure is made under section 54 (Bill 6–EN para. 88).

14.6.4 Common law duties

Section 54(9) of the Act recognises that other common law and statutory powers permitting disclosure may apply. These will stand alongside the section 54 duty imposed upon individuals making disclosure.

The government have concluded, however, 'that the existence of a statutory authority to disclose will be sufficient to override common law duties' of confidentiality (Baroness Scotland, House of Lords, Hansard, col. 1453, 11 March 2004).

14.7 GRANTS FOR ASSISTING VICTIMS, WITNESSES etc.

Section 56(1) of the Act provides statutory authority for the Home Secretary to pay government grants for bodies that assist victims, witnesses or others affected by offences, including children. This is intended to ensure that regular government grants, to which conditions may be attached (s.56(2)), can be paid, at the Home Secretary's discretion, to voluntary sector bodies to which grants may already be paid informally. It does not signal that more funding is available nor that funding will be redistributed.

PART V **MATERIALS**

Appendix
DOMESTIC VIOLENCE, CRIME AND VICTIMS ACT 2004

2004 CHAPTER 28

CONTENTS

PART 1 DOMESTIC VIOLENCE ETC

PART 2 CRIMINAL JUSTICE

CHAPTER 3 OTHER MATTERS RELATING TO VICTIMS ETC

Parliamentary Commissioner

47 Investigations by Parliamentary Commissioner

Commissioner for Victims and Witnesses

48 Commissioner for Victims and Witnesses
49 General functions of Commissioner
50 Advice
51 Restrictions on exercise of functions
52 'Victims' and 'witnesses'
53 Authorities within Commissioner's remit

Disclosure of information

54 Disclosure of information

Victims' Advisory Panel

55 Victims' Advisory Panel

Grants

56 Grants for assisting victims, witnesses etc

Criminal injuries compensation

57 Recovery of criminal injuries compensation from offenders

PART 4 SUPPLEMENTARY

58 Amendments and repeals
59 Transitional and transitory provisions
60 Commencement
61 Orders
62 Extent
63 Short title

Schedule 1 – Modification of sections 17 to 20 for Northern Ireland
Schedule 2 – Supervision orders on finding of insanity or unfitness to plead etc
Schedule 3 – Unfitness to stand trial and insanity: courts-martial etc
Schedule 4 – Powers of authorised officers executing warrants
Schedule 5 – Procedure on breach of community penalty etc
Schedule 6 – Intermittent custody
Schedule 7 – Investigations by Parliamentary Commissioner
Schedule 8 – Commissioner for Victims and Witnesses
Schedule 9 – Authorities within Commissioner's remit
Schedule 10 – Minor and consequential amendments
Schedule 11 – Repeals
Schedule 12 – Transitional and transitory provisions

An Act to amend Part 4 of the Family Law Act 1996, the Protection from Harassment Act 1997 and the Protection from Harassment (Northern Ireland) Order 1997; to make provision about homicide; to make common assault an arrestable offence; to make provision for the payment of surcharges by offenders; to make provision about alternative verdicts; to provide for a procedure under which a jury tries only sample counts on an indictment; to make provision about findings of unfitness to plead and about persons found unfit to plead or not guilty by reason of insanity; to make provision about the execution of warrants; to make provision about the enforcement of orders imposed on conviction; to amend section 58 of the Criminal Justice Act 2003 and to amend Part 12 of that Act in relation to intermittent custody; to make provision in relation to victims of offences, witnesses of offences and others affected by offences; and to make provision about the recovery of compensation from offenders.

[15th November 2004]

BE IT ENACTED by the Queen's most Excellent Majesty, by and with the advice and consent of the Lords Spiritual and Temporal, and Commons, in this present Parliament assembled, and by the authority of the same, as follows:

PART 1 DOMESTIC VIOLENCE ETC

Amendments to Part 4 of the Family Law Act 1996

1 Breach of non-molestation order to be a criminal offence

In Part 4 of the Family Law Act 1996 (c. 27) (family homes and domestic violence), after section 42 insert –

> '**42A Offence of breaching non-molestation order**
>
> (1) A person who without reasonable excuse does anything that he is prohibited from doing by a non-molestation order is guilty of an offence.
>
> (2) In the case of a non-molestation order made by virtue of section 45(1), a person can be guilty of an offence under this section only in respect of conduct engaged in at a time when he was aware of the existence of the order.
>
> (3) Where a person is convicted of an offence under this section in respect of any conduct, that conduct is not punishable as a contempt of court.
>
> (4) A person cannot be convicted of an offence under this section in respect of any conduct which has been punished as a contempt of court.
>
> (5) A person guilty of an offence under this section is liable –
>
> (a) on conviction on indictment, to imprisonment for a term not exceeding five years, or a fine, or both;
>
> (b) on summary conviction, to imprisonment for a term not exceeding 12 months, or a fine not exceeding the statutory maximum, or both.
>
> (6) A reference in any enactment to proceedings under this Part, or to an order under this Part, does not include a reference to proceedings for an offence under this section or to an order made in such proceedings.
>
> "Enactment" includes an enactment contained in subordinate legislation within the meaning of the Interpretation Act 1978 (c. 30).'

2 Additional considerations if parties are cohabitants or former cohabitants

(1) Section 41 of the Family Law Act 1996 (c. 27) (which requires a court, when considering the nature of the relationship of cohabitants or former cohabitants, to have regard to their non-married status) is repealed.

(2) In section 36(6)(e) of that Act (court to have regard to nature of parties' relationship when considering whether to give right to occupy to cohabitant or former cohabitant with no existing right), after 'relationship' insert 'and in particular the level of commitment involved in it'.

3 'Cohabitants' in Part 4 of 1996 Act to include same-sex couples

In section 62(1)(a) of the Family Law Act 1996 (definition of 'cohabitant' for the purposes of Part 4 of that Act), for the words after '"cohabitants" are' substitute 'two persons who, although not married to each other, are living together as husband and wife or (if of the same sex) in an equivalent relationship; and'.

4 Extension of Part 4 of 1996 Act to non-cohabiting couples

In section 62(3) of the Family Law Act 1996 (definition of 'associated' persons for the purposes of Part 4 of that Act), after paragraph (e) insert –

'(ea) they have or have had an intimate personal relationship with each other which is or was of significant duration;'.

Causing or allowing the death of a child or vulnerable adult

5 The offence

(1) A person ('D') is guilty of an offence if –

(a) a child or vulnerable adult ('V') dies as a result of the unlawful act of a person who –

(i) was a member of the same household as V, and
(ii) had frequent contact with him,

(b) D was such a person at the time of that act,
(c) at that time there was a significant risk of serious physical harm being caused to V by the unlawful act of such a person, and
(d) either D was the person whose act caused V's death or –

(i) D was, or ought to have been, aware of the risk mentioned in paragraph (c),
(ii) D failed to take such steps as he could reasonably have been expected to take to protect V from the risk, and
(iii) the act occurred in circumstances of the kind that D foresaw or ought to have foreseen.

(2) The prosecution does not have to prove whether it is the first alternative in subsection (1)(d) or the second (sub-paragraphs (i) to (iii)) that applies.
(3) If D was not the mother or father of V –

(a) D may not be charged with an offence under this section if he was under the age of 16 at the time of the act that caused V's death;
(b) for the purposes of subsection (1)(d)(ii) D could not have been expected to take any such step as is referred to there before attaining that age.

(4) For the purposes of this section –

(a) a person is to be regarded as a 'member' of a particular household, even if he does not live in that household, if he visits it so often and for such periods of time that it is reasonable to regard him as a member of it;
(b) where V lived in different households at different times, 'the same household as V' refers to the household in which V was living at the time of the act that caused V's death.

(5) For the purposes of this section an 'unlawful' act is one that –

(a) constitutes an offence, or
(b) would constitute an offence but for being the act of –

(i) a person under the age of ten, or
(ii) a person entitled to rely on a defence of insanity.

Paragraph (b) does not apply to an act of D.

(6) In this section –

'act' includes a course of conduct and also includes omission;
'child' means a person under the age of 16;
'serious' harm means harm that amounts to grievous bodily harm for the purposes of the Offences against the Person Act 1861 (c. 100);
'vulnerable adult' means a person aged 16 or over whose ability to protect himself from violence, abuse or neglect is significantly impaired through physical or mental disability or illness, through old age or otherwise.

(7) A person guilty of an offence under this section is liable on conviction on indictment to imprisonment for a term not exceeding 14 years or to a fine, or to both.

6 Evidence and procedure: England and Wales

(1) Subsections (2) to (4) apply where a person ('the defendant') is charged in the same proceedings with an offence of murder or manslaughter and with an offence under section 5 in respect of the same death ('the section 5 offence').
(2) Where by virtue of section 35(3) of the Criminal Justice and Public Order Act 1994 (c. 33) a court or jury is permitted, in relation to the section 5 offence, to draw such inferences as appear proper from the defendant's failure to give evidence or refusal to answer a question, the court or jury may also draw such inferences in determining whether he is guilty –

(a) of murder or manslaughter, or
(b) of any other offence of which he could lawfully be convicted on the charge of murder or manslaughter,

even if there would otherwise be no case for him to answer in relation to that offence.
(3) The charge of murder or manslaughter is not to be dismissed under paragraph 2 of Schedule 3 to the Crime and Disorder Act 1998 (c. 37) (unless the section 5 offence is dismissed).
(4) At the defendant's trial the question whether there is a case for the defendant to answer on the charge of murder or manslaughter is not to be considered before the close of all the evidence (or, if at some earlier time he ceases to be charged with the section 5 offence, before that earlier time).
(5) An offence under section 5 is an offence of homicide for the purposes of the following enactments –

sections 24 and 25 of the Magistrates' Courts Act 1980 (c. 43) (mode of trial of child or young person for indictable offence);
section 51A of the Crime and Disorder Act 1998 (sending cases to the Crown Court: children and young persons);
section 8 of the Powers of Criminal Courts (Sentencing) Act 2000 (c. 6) (power and duty to remit young offenders to youth courts for sentence).

7 Evidence and procedure: Northern Ireland

(1) Subsections (2) to (4) apply where a person ('the defendant') is charged in the same proceedings with an offence of murder or manslaughter and with an offence under section 5 in respect of the same death ('the section 5 offence').
(2) Where by virtue of Article 4(4) of the Criminal Evidence (Northern Ireland) Order 1988 (S.I. 1988/1987 (N.I. 20)) a court or jury is permitted, in relation to the section 5 offence, to draw such inferences as appear proper from the defendant's failure to give evidence or refusal to answer a question, the court or jury may also draw such inferences in determining whether he is guilty –

(a) of murder or manslaughter, or
(b) of any other offence of which he could lawfully be convicted on the charge of murder or manslaughter,

even if there would otherwise be no case for him to answer in relation to that offence.

(3) Where a magistrates' court is considering under Article 37 of the Magistrates' Courts (Northern Ireland) Order 1981 (S.I. 1981/1675 (N.I. 26)) whether to commit the defendant for trial for the offence of murder or manslaughter, if there is sufficient evidence to put him upon trial for the section 5 offence there is deemed to be sufficient evidence to put him upon trial for the offence of murder or manslaughter.

(4) At the defendant's trial the question whether there is a case to answer on the charge of murder or manslaughter is not to be considered before the close of all the evidence (or, if at some earlier time he ceases to be charged with the section 5 offence, before that earlier time).

(5) An offence under section 5 is an offence of homicide for the purposes of the following provisions –

Article 17 of the Criminal Justice (Children) (Northern Ireland) Order 1998 (S.I. 1998/1504 (N.I. 9)) (mode of trial of child for indictable offence);

Article 32 of that Order (power and duty to remit children to youth courts for sentence).

8 Evidence and procedure: courts-martial

(1) Section 6(1), (2) and (4) has effect in relation to proceedings before courts-martial with the following adaptations.

(2) A reference to an offence of murder or manslaughter or an offence under section 5 is to be read as a reference to an offence under –

(a) section 70 of the Army Act 1955 (3 & 4 Eliz. 2 c. 18),
(b) section 70 of the Air Force Act 1955 (3 & 4 Eliz. 2 c. 19), or
(c) section 42 of the Naval Discipline Act 1957 (c. 53),

for which the offence referred to in section 6 is the corresponding civil offence (within the meaning of that Act).

(3) A reference to the court or jury is to be read as a reference to the court.

Domestic homicide reviews

9 Establishment and conduct of reviews

(1) In this section 'domestic homicide review' means a review of the circumstances in which the death of a person aged 16 or over has, or appears to have, resulted from violence, abuse or neglect by –

(a) a person to whom he was related or with whom he was or had been in an intimate personal relationship, or
(b) a member of the same household as himself,

held with a view to identifying the lessons to be learnt from the death.

(2) The Secretary of State may in a particular case direct a specified person or body within subsection (4) to establish, or to participate in, a domestic homicide review.

(3) It is the duty of any person or body within subsection (4) establishing or participating in a domestic homicide review (whether or not held pursuant to a direction under subsection (2)) to have regard to any guidance issued by the Secretary of State as to the establishment and conduct of such reviews.

(4) The persons and bodies within this subsection are –

(a) in relation to England and Wales –
chief officers of police for police areas in England and Wales;
local authorities;
local probation boards established under section 4 of the Criminal Justice and Court Services Act 2000 (c. 43);
Strategic Health Authorities established under section 8 of the National Health Service Act 1977 (c. 49);

Primary Care Trusts established under Section 16A of that Act.
Local Health Boards established under section 16BA of that Act;
NHS trusts established under section 5 of the National Health Service and Community Care Act 1990 (c. 19);

(b) in relation to Northern Ireland –
the Chief Constable of the Police Service of Northern Ireland;
the Probation Board for Northern Ireland;
Health and Social Services Boards established under Article 16 of the Health and Personal Social Services (Northern Ireland) Order 1972 (S.I. 1972/1265 (N.I. 14));
Health and Social Services trusts established under Article 10 of the Health and Personal Social Services (Northern Ireland) Order 1991 (S.I. 1991/194 (N.I. 1)).

(5) In subsection (4)(a) 'local authority' means –

(a) in relation to England, the council of a district, county or London borough, the Common Council of the City of London and the Council of the Isles of Scilly;
(b) in relation to Wales, the council of a county or county borough.

(6) The Secretary of State may by order amend subsection (4) or (5).

PART 2 CRIMINAL JUSTICE

Assault, harassment etc

10 Common assault to be an arrestable offence

(1) In Schedule 1A to the Police and Criminal Evidence Act 1984 (c. 60) (specific offences which are arrestable offences), before paragraph 15 (but after the heading '*Criminal Justice Act 1988*') insert –

'14A Common assault.'

(2) In Article 26(2) of the Police and Criminal Evidence (Northern Ireland) Order 1989 (S.I. 1989/1341 (N.I. 12)) (specific offences which are arrestable offences), after paragraph (m) insert –

'(n) an offence under section 42 of the Offences against the Person Act 1861 (c. 100) (common assault etc).'

11 Common assault etc as alternative verdict

In section 6 of the Criminal Law Act 1967 (c. 58) (trial of offences), after subsection (3) (alternative verdicts on trial on indictment) insert –

'(3A) For the purposes of subsection (3) above an offence falls within the jurisdiction of the court of trial if it is an offence to which section 40 of the Criminal Justice Act 1988 applies (power to join in indictment count for common assault etc.), even if a count charging the offence is not included in the indictment.

(3B) A person convicted of an offence by virtue of subsection (3A) may only be dealt with for it in a manner in which a magistrates' court could have dealt with him.'

12 Restraining orders: England and Wales

(1) In section 5 of the Protection from Harassment Act 1997 (c. 40) (power to make restraining order where defendant convicted of offence under section 2 or 4 of that Act), in subsection (1) omit 'under section 2 or 4'.

(2) After subsection (3) of that section insert –

'(3A) In proceedings under this section both the prosecution and the defence may lead, as further evidence, any evidence that would be admissible in proceedings for an injunction under section 3.'

(3) After subsection (4) of that section insert –

'(4A) Any person mentioned in the order is entitled to be heard on the hearing of an application under subsection (4).'

(4) After subsection (6) of that section insert –

'(7) A court dealing with a person for an offence under this section may vary or discharge the order in question by a further order.'

(5) After that section insert –

'5A Restraining orders on acquittal

(1) A court before which a person ("the defendant") is acquitted of an offence may, if it considers it necessary to do so to protect a person from harassment by the defendant, make an order prohibiting the defendant from doing anything described in the order.
(2) Subsections (3) to (7) of section 5 apply to an order under this section as they apply to an order under that one.
(3) Where the Court of Appeal allow an appeal against conviction they may remit the case to the Crown Court to consider whether to proceed under this section.
(4) Where –

(a) the Crown Court allows an appeal against conviction, or
(b) a case is remitted to the Crown Court under subsection (3),

the reference in subsection (1) to a court before which a person is acquitted of an offence is to be read as referring to that court.
(5) A person made subject to an order under this section has the same right of appeal against the order as if –

(a) he had been convicted of the offence in question before the court which made the order, and
(b) the order had been made under section 5.'

13 Restraining orders: Northern Ireland

(1) In Article 7 of the Protection from Harassment (Northern Ireland) Order 1997 (S.I. 1997/1180 (N.I. 9)) (power to make restraining order where defendant convicted of offence under Article 4 or 6 of that Order), in paragraph (1) omit 'under Article 4 or 6'.
(2) After paragraph (3) of that Article insert –

'(3A) In proceedings under this Article both the prosecution and the defence may lead, as further evidence, any evidence that would be admissible in proceedings for an injunction under Article 5.'

(3) After paragraph (4) of that Article insert –

'(4A) Any person mentioned in the order is entitled to be heard on the hearing of an application under paragraph (4).'

(4) After paragraph (6) of that Article insert –

'(7) A court dealing with a person for an offence under this Article may vary or discharge the order in question by a further order.'

(5) After that Article insert –

'7A Restraining orders on acquittal

(1) A court before which a person ("the defendant") is acquitted of an offence may, if it considers it necessary to do so to protect a person from harassment by the

defendant, make an order prohibiting the defendant from doing anything described in the order.

(2) Paragraphs (3) to (7) of Article 7 apply to an order under this Article as they apply to an order under that one.

(3) Where the Court of Appeal allow an appeal against conviction they may remit the case to the Crown Court to consider whether to proceed under this Article.

(4) Where –

(a) a county court allows an appeal against conviction, or

(b) a case is remitted to the Crown Court under paragraph (3),

the reference in paragraph (1) to a court before which a person is acquitted of an offence is to be read as referring to that court.

(5) A person made subject to an order under this Article has the same right of appeal against the order as if –

(a) he had been convicted of the offence in question before the court which made the order, and

(b) the order had been made under Article 7.'

Surcharges

14 Surcharge payable on conviction

(1) In Chapter 1 of Part 12 of the Criminal Justice Act 2003 (c. 44) (general provisions about sentencing), after section 161 insert –

'Surcharges

161A Court's duty to order payment of surcharge

(1) A court when dealing with a person for one or more offences must also (subject to subsections (2) and (3)) order him to pay a surcharge.

(2) Subsection (1) does not apply in such cases as may be prescribed by an order made by the Secretary of State.

(3) Where a court dealing with an offender considers –

(a) that it would be appropriate to make a compensation order, but

(b) that he has insufficient means to pay both the surcharge and appropriate compensation,

the court must reduce the surcharge accordingly (if necessary to nil).

(4) For the purposes of this section a court does not "deal with" a person if it –

(a) discharges him absolutely, or

(b) makes an order under the Mental Health Act 1983 in respect of him.

161B Amount of surcharge

(1) The surcharge payable under section 161A is such amount as the Secretary of State may specify by order.

(2) An order under this section may provide for the amount to depend on –

(a) the offence or offences committed,

(b) how the offender is otherwise dealt with (including, where the offender is fined, the amount of the fine),

(c) the age of the offender.

This is not to be read as limiting section 330(3) (power to make different provision for different purposes etc).'

(2) In section 164 of that Act (fixing of fines), after subsection (4) insert –

'(4A) In applying subsection (3), a court must not reduce the amount of a fine on account of any surcharge it orders the offender to pay under section 161A, except to the extent that he has insufficient means to pay both.'

(3) In Part 1 of Schedule 9 to the Administration of Justice Act 1970 (c. 31) (cases where payment enforceable as on summary conviction), after paragraph 12 insert –

'13 Where under section 161A of the Criminal Justice Act 2003 a court orders the payment of a surcharge.'

(4) In Schedule 5 to the Courts Act 2003 (c. 39) (collection of fines), in paragraph 1(1) (application of Schedule), after 'a fine' insert 'or a surcharge imposed under section 161A of the Criminal Justice Act 2003'.

(5) The Secretary of State may by order –

(a) make provision amending Schedule 5 (collection of fines) or Schedule 6 (discharge of fines by unpaid work) to the Courts Act 2003 in its application by virtue of subsection (3) or (4) to surcharges;
(b) make provision for any part of Schedule 5, or the whole or any part of Schedule 6, not to apply to surcharges;
(c) make amendments to any enactment that are consequential on provision made under paragraph (a) or (b).

15 Increase in maximum on-the-spot penalty for disorderly behaviour

(1) In Chapter 1 of Part 1 of the Criminal Justice and Police Act 2001 (c. 16) (on-the-spot penalties for disorderly behaviour), section 3 is amended as follows.

(2) In subsection (2) (maximum penalty that may be prescribed), at the end insert 'plus a half of the relevant surcharge'.

(3) After that subsection insert –

'(2A) The "relevant surcharge", in relation to a person of a given age, is the amount payable by way of surcharge under section 161A of the Criminal Justice Act 2003 by a person of that age who is fined the maximum amount for the offence.'

16 Higher fixed penalty for repeated road traffic offences

(1) The Road Traffic Offenders Act 1988 (c. 53) is amended as follows.

(2) In section 53 (amount of fixed penalty), after subsection (2) insert –

'(3) In particular, in relation to England and Wales an order made under subsection (1)(a) may prescribe a higher fixed penalty in a case where, in the period of three years ending with the date of the offence in question, the offender committed an offence for which –

(a) he was disqualified from driving, or
(b) penalty points were endorsed on the counterpart of any licence held by him.'

(3) At the end of section 84 (regulations) (which becomes subsection (1)) insert –

'(2) The Secretary of State may by regulations provide that where –

(a) a conditional offer has been issued under section 75 of this Act,
(b) the amount of the penalty stated in the offer is not the higher amount applicable by virtue of section 53(3) of this Act, and
(c) it subsequently appears that that higher amount is in fact applicable,

the fixed penalty clerk may issue a further notice (a "surcharge notice") requiring payment of the difference between the two amounts.

(3) Regulations under subsection (2) above may –

(a) provide for this Part of this Act to have effect, in cases to which the regulations apply, with such modifications as may be specified;

(b) make provision for the collection and enforcement of amounts due under surcharge notices.'

Trial by jury of sample counts only

17 Application by prosecution for certain counts to be tried without a jury

(1) The prosecution may apply to a judge of the Crown Court for a trial on indictment to take place on the basis that the trial of some, but not all, of the counts included in the indictment may be conducted without a jury.

(2) If such an application is made and the judge is satisfied that the following three conditions are fulfilled, he may make an order for the trial to take place on the basis that the trial of some, but not all, of the counts included in the indictment may be conducted without a jury.

(3) The first condition is that the number of counts included in the indictment is likely to mean that a trial by jury involving all of those counts would be impracticable.

(4) The second condition is that, if an order under subsection (2) were made, each count or group of counts which would accordingly be tried with a jury can be regarded as a sample of counts which could accordingly be tried without a jury.

(5) The third condition is that it is in the interests of justice for an order under subsection (2) to be made.

(6) In deciding whether or not to make an order under subsection (2), the judge must have regard to any steps which might reasonably be taken to facilitate a trial by jury.

(7) But a step is not to be regarded as reasonable if it could lead to the possibility of a defendant in the trial receiving a lesser sentence than would be the case if that step were not taken.

(8) An order under subsection (2) must specify the counts which may be tried without a jury.

(9) For the purposes of this section and sections 18 to 20, a count may not be regarded as a sample of other counts unless the defendant in respect of each count is the same person.

18 Procedure for applications under section 17

(1) An application under section 17 must be determined at a preparatory hearing.

(2) Section 7(1) of the 1987 Act and section 29(2) of the 1996 Act are to have effect as if the purposes there mentioned included the purpose of determining an application under section 17.

(3) Section 29(1) of the 1996 Act is to have effect as if the grounds on which a judge of the Crown Court may make an order under that provision included the ground that an application under section 17 has been made.

(4) The parties to a preparatory hearing at which an application under section 17 is to be determined must be given an opportunity to make representations with respect to the application.

(5) Section 9(11) of the 1987 Act and section 35(1) of the 1996 Act are to have effect as if they also provided for an appeal to the Court of Appeal to lie from the determination by a judge of an application under section 17.

(6) In this section –

'preparatory hearing' means a preparatory hearing within the meaning of the 1987 Act or Part 3 of the 1996 Act;

'the 1987 Act' means the Criminal Justice Act 1987 (c. 38);

'the 1996 Act' means the Criminal Procedure and Investigations Act 1996 (c. 25).

19 Effect of order under section 17(2)

(1) The effect of an order under section 17(2) is that where, in the course of the proceedings to which the order relates, a defendant is found guilty by a jury on a count

which can be regarded as a sample of other counts to be tried in those proceedings, those other counts may be tried without a jury in those proceedings.

(2) Where the trial of a count is conducted without a jury because of an order under section 17(2), the court is to have all the powers, authorities and jurisdiction which the court would have had if the trial of that count had been conducted with a jury (including power to determine any question and to make any finding which would be required to be determined or made by a jury).

(3) Except where the context otherwise requires, any reference in an enactment to a jury, the verdict of a jury or the finding of a jury is to be read, in relation to the trial of a count conducted without a jury because of an order under section 17(2), as a reference to the court, the verdict of the court or the finding of the court.

(4) Where the trial of a count is conducted without a jury because of an order under section 17(2) and the court convicts the defendant of that count –

(a) the court must give a judgment which states the reasons for the conviction at, or as soon as reasonably practicable after, the time of the conviction, and

(b) the reference in section 18(2) of the Criminal Appeal Act 1968 (c. 19) (notice of appeal or of application for leave to appeal to be given within 28 days from date of conviction etc) to the date of the conviction is to be read as a reference to the date of the judgment mentioned in paragraph (a).

(5) Where, in the case of proceedings in respect of which an order under section 17(2) has been made, a jury convicts a defendant of a count, time does not begin to run under section 18(2) of the Criminal Appeal Act 1968 in relation to an appeal against that conviction until the date on which the proceedings end.

(6) In determining for the purposes of subsection (5) the date on which proceedings end, any part of those proceedings which takes place after the time when matters relating to sentencing begin to be dealt with is to be disregarded.

(7) Nothing in this section or section 17, 18 or 20 affects the requirement under section 4A of the Criminal Procedure (Insanity) Act 1964 (c. 84) that any question, finding or verdict mentioned in that section be determined, made or returned by a jury.

20 Rules of court

(1) Rules of court may make such provision as appears to the authority making them to be necessary or expedient for the purposes of sections 17 to 19.

(2) Without limiting subsection (1), rules of court may in particular make provision for time limits within which applications under section 17 must be made or within which other things in connection with that section or section 18 or 19 must be done.

(3) Nothing in this section is to be taken as affecting the generality of any enactment conferring powers to make rules of court.

21 Application of sections 17 to 20 to Northern Ireland

(1) In their application to Northern Ireland, sections 17 to 20 have effect subject to the modifications in Schedule 1.

(2) Sections 17 to 20 do not apply in relation to a trial to which section 75 of the Terrorism Act 2000 (c. 11) (trial without jury for certain offences) applies.

Unfitness to plead and insanity

22 Procedure for determining fitness to plead: England and Wales

(1) The Criminal Procedure (Insanity) Act 1964 is amended as follows.

(2) In section 4 (finding of unfitness to plead), in subsection (5) (question of fitness to be determined by a jury), for the words from 'by a jury' to the end substitute 'by the court without a jury'.

(3) In subsection (6) of that section, for 'A jury' substitute 'The court'.
(4) In subsection (1) of section 4A (finding that the accused did the act or omission charged against him), for 'jury' substitute 'court'.
(5) For subsection (5) of that section substitute –

'(5) Where the question of disability was determined after arraignment of the accused, the determination under subsection (2) is to be made by the jury by whom he was being tried.'

23 Procedure for determining fitness to be tried: Northern Ireland

(1) The Mental Health (Northern Ireland) Order 1986 (S.I. 1986/595 (N.I. 4)) is amended as follows.
(2) In Article 49 (finding of unfitness to be tried), in paragraph (4) (question of fitness to be determined by a jury), for the words from 'by a jury' to the end substitute 'by the court without a jury'.
(3) In paragraph (4A) of that Article, for 'A jury' substitute 'The court'.
(4) In paragraph (1) of Article 49A (finding that the accused did the act or omission charged against him), for 'jury' substitute 'court'.
(5) For paragraph (5) of that Article substitute –

'(5) Where the question of fitness to be tried was determined after arraignment of the accused, the determination under paragraph (2) is to be made by the jury by whom he was being tried.'

24 Powers of court on finding of insanity or unfitness to plead etc

(1) For section 5 of the Criminal Procedure (Insanity) Act 1964 (c. 84) substitute –

'5 Powers to deal with persons not guilty by reason of insanity or unfit to plead etc.

(1) This section applies where –

(a) a special verdict is returned that the accused is not guilty by reason of insanity; or
(b) findings have been made that the accused is under a disability and that he did the act or made the omission charged against him.

(2) The court shall make in respect of the accused –

(a) a hospital order (with or without a restriction order);
(b) a supervision order; or
(c) an order for his absolute discharge.

(3) Where –

(a) the offence to which the special verdict or the findings relate is an offence the sentence for which is fixed by law, and
(b) the court have power to make a hospital order,

the court shall make a hospital order with a restriction order (whether or not they would have power to make a restriction order apart from this subsection).

(4) In this section –

"hospital order" has the meaning given in section 37 of the Mental Health Act 1983;
"restriction order" has the meaning given to it by section 41 of that Act;
"supervision order" has the meaning given in Part 1 of Schedule 1A to this Act.

5A Orders made under or by virtue of section 5

(1) In relation to the making of an order by virtue of subsection (2)(a) of section 5 above, section 37 (hospital orders etc) of the Mental Health Act 1983 ("the 1983 Act") shall have effect as if –

(a) the reference in subsection (1) to a person being convicted before the Crown Court included a reference to the case where section 5 above applies;
(b) the words after "punishable with imprisonment" and before "or is convicted" were omitted; and
(c) for subsections (4) and (5) there were substituted –

"(4) Where an order is made under this section requiring a person to be admitted to a hospital ('a hospital order'), it shall be the duty of the managers of the hospital specified in the order to admit him in accordance with it."

(2) In relation to a case where section 5 above applies but the court have not yet made one of the disposals mentioned in subsection (2) of that section –

(a) section 35 of the 1983 Act (remand to hospital for report on accused's mental condition) shall have effect with the omission of the words after paragraph (b) in subsection (3);
(b) section 36 of that Act (remand of accused person to hospital for treatment) shall have effect with the omission of the words "(other than an offence the sentence for which is fixed by law)" in subsection (2);
(c) references in sections 35 and 36 of that Act to an accused person shall be construed as including a person in whose case this subsection applies; and
(d) section 38 of that Act (interim hospital orders) shall have effect as if –

(i) the reference in subsection (1) to a person being convicted before the Crown Court included a reference to the case where section 5 above applies; and
(ii) the words "(other than an offence the sentence for which is fixed by law)" in that subsection were omitted.

(3) In relation to the making of any order under the 1983 Act by virtue of this Act, references in the 1983 Act to an offender shall be construed as including references to a person in whose case section 5 above applies, and references to an offence shall be construed accordingly.

(4) Where –

(a) a person is detained in pursuance of a hospital order which the court had power to make by virtue of section 5(1)(b) above, and
(b) the court also made a restriction order, and that order has not ceased to have effect,

the Secretary of State, if satisfied after consultation with the responsible medical officer that the person can properly be tried, may remit the person for trial, either to the court of trial or to a prison.

On the person's arrival at the court or prison, the hospital order and the restriction order shall cease to have effect.

(5) Schedule 1A to this Act (supervision orders) has effect with respect to the making of supervision orders under subsection (2)(b) of section 5 above, and with respect to the revocation and amendment of such orders.

(6) In relation to the making of an order under subsection (2)(c) of section 5 above, section 12(1) of the Powers of Criminal Courts (Sentencing) Act 2000 (absolute and conditional discharge) shall have effect as if –

(a) the reference to a person being convicted by or before a court of such an offence as is there mentioned included a reference to the case where section 5 above applies; and
(b) the reference to the court being of opinion that it is inexpedient to inflict punishment included a reference to it thinking that an order for absolute discharge would be most suitable in all the circumstances of the case.'

(2) Before Schedule 2 to the Criminal Procedure (Insanity) Act 1964 (c. 84) insert the Schedule set out in Schedule 2 to this Act.

(3) In section 6 of the Criminal Appeal Act 1968 (c. 19) (substitution of finding of insanity or findings of unfitness to plead etc) and in section 14 of that Act (substitution of findings of unfitness to plead etc), for subsections (2) and (3) substitute –

'(2) The Court of Appeal shall make in respect of the accused –

(a) a hospital order (with or without a restriction order);
(b) a supervision order; or
(c) an order for his absolute discharge.

(3) Where –

(a) the offence to which the appeal relates is an offence the sentence for which is fixed by law, and
(b) the court have power to make a hospital order,

the court shall make a hospital order with a restriction order (whether or not they would have power to make a restriction order apart from this subsection).

(4) Section 5A of the Criminal Procedure (Insanity) Act 1964 ("the 1964 Act") applies in relation to this section as it applies in relation to section 5 of that Act.

(5) Where the Court of Appeal make an interim hospital order by virtue of this section –

(a) the power of renewing or terminating it and of dealing with the appellant on its termination shall be exercisable by the court below and not by the Court of Appeal; and
(b) the court below shall be treated for the purposes of section 38(7) of the Mental Health Act 1983 (absconding offenders) as the court that made the order.

(6) Where the Court of Appeal make a supervision order by virtue of this section, any power of revoking or amending it shall be exercisable as if the order had been made by the court below.

(7) In this section –

"hospital order" has the meaning given in section 37 of the Mental Health Act 1983;
"interim hospital order" has the meaning given in section 38 of that Act;
"restriction order" has the meaning given to it by section 41 of that Act;
"supervision order" has the meaning given in Part 1 of Schedule 1A to the 1964 Act.'

(4) Section 14A of the Criminal Appeal Act 1968 (c. 19) (power to order admission to hospital where, on appeal against verdict of not guilty by reason of insanity, Court of Appeal substitutes verdict of acquittal) is repealed.

(5) Section 5 of the Criminal Procedure (Insanity and Unfitness to Plead) Act 1991 (c. 25) and Schedules 1 and 2 to that Act are repealed.

25 Appeal against order made on finding of insanity or unfitness to plead etc

After section 16 of the Criminal Appeal Act 1968 insert –

'Appeal against order made in cases of insanity or unfitness to plead

16A Right of appeal against hospital order etc.

(1) A person in whose case the Crown Court –

(a) makes a hospital order or interim hospital order by virtue of section 5 or 5A of the Criminal Procedure (Insanity) Act 1964, or
(b) makes a supervision order under section 5 of that Act,

may appeal to the Court of Appeal against the order.

(2) An appeal under this section lies only –

(a) with the leave of the Court of Appeal; or

(b) if the judge of the court of trial grants a certificate that the case is fit for appeal.

16B Disposal of appeal under s.16A

(1) If on an appeal under section 16A of this Act the Court of Appeal consider that the appellant should be dealt with differently from the way in which the court below dealt with him –

(a) they may quash any order which is the subject of the appeal; and

(b) they may make such order, whether by substitution for the original order or by variation of or addition to it, as they think appropriate for the case and as the court below had power to make.

(2) The fact that an appeal is pending against an interim hospital order under the Mental Health Act 1983 shall not affect the power of the court below to renew or terminate the order or deal with the appellant on its termination.

(3) Where the Court of Appeal make an interim hospital order by virtue of this section –

(a) the power of renewing or terminating it and of dealing with the appellant on its termination shall be exercisable by the court below and not by the Court of Appeal; and

(b) the court below shall be treated for the purposes of section 38(7) of the said Act of 1983 (absconding offenders) as the court that made the order.

(4) The fact that an appeal is pending against a supervision order under section 5 of the Criminal Procedure (Insanity) Act 1964 shall not affect the power of the court below to revoke the order, or of a magistrates' court to revoke or amend it.

(5) Where the Court of Appeal make a supervision order by virtue of this section, the power of revoking or amending it shall be exercisable as if the order had been made by the court below.'

26 Courts-martial etc

Schedule 3 (unfitness to stand trial and insanity: courts-martial etc) has effect.

Miscellaneous

27 Powers of authorised officers executing warrants

(1) After section 125B of the Magistrates' Courts Act 1980 (c. 43) insert –

'125BA Powers of persons authorised under section 125A or 125B

Schedule 4A to this Act, which confers powers on persons authorised under section 125A or 125B for the purpose of executing warrants for the enforcement of fines and other orders, shall have effect.'

(2) After Schedule 4 to that Act insert the Schedule set out in Schedule 4 to this Act.

28 Disclosure orders for purpose of executing warrants

After section 125C of the Magistrates' Courts Act 1980 insert –

'125CA Power to make disclosure order

(1) A magistrates' court may make a disclosure order if satisfied that it is necessary to do so for the purpose of executing a warrant to which this section applies.

(2) This section applies to a warrant of arrest, commitment, detention or distress issued by a justice of the peace in connection with the enforcement of a fine or other order imposed or made on conviction.
(3) A disclosure order is an order requiring the person to whom it is directed to supply the designated officer for the court with any of the following information about the person to whom the warrant relates –
  (a) his name, date of birth or national insurance number;
  (b) his address (or any of his addresses).
(4) A disclosure order may be made only on the application of a person entitled to execute the warrant.
(5) This section applies to the Crown as it applies to other persons.

125CB Use of information supplied under disclosure order

(1) Information supplied to a person under a disclosure order, or under this subsection, may be supplied by him to –
  (a) the applicant for the order or any other person entitled to execute the warrant concerned;
  (b) any employee of a body or person who, for the purposes of section 125B above, is an approved enforcement agency in relation to the warrant;
  (c) any justices' clerk or other person appointed under section 2(1) of the Courts Act 2003.
(2) A person who intentionally or recklessly –
  (a) discloses information supplied under a disclosure order otherwise than as permitted by subsection (1) above, or
  (b) uses information so supplied otherwise than for the purpose of facilitating the execution of the warrant concerned,

  commits an offence.
(3) But it is not an offence under subsection (2) above –
  (a) to disclose any information in accordance with any enactment or order of a court or for the purposes of any proceedings before a court; or
  (b) to disclose any information which has previously been lawfully disclosed to the public.
(4) A person guilty of an offence under subsection (2) above is liable –
  (a) on summary conviction, to a fine not exceeding the statutory maximum;
  (b) on conviction on indictment, to a fine.
(5) In this section "disclosure order" has the meaning given by section 125CA(3) above.'

29 Procedure on breach of community penalty etc

Schedule 5 (procedure on breach of community penalty etc) has effect.

30 Prosecution appeals

(1) In section 58(13) of the Criminal Justice Act 2003 (c. 44) (which defines 'applicable time'), for 'start of the judge's' substitute 'time when the judge starts his'.
(2) After section 58(13) of that Act insert –

  '(14) The reference in subsection (13) to the time when the judge starts his summing-up to the jury includes the time when the judge would start his summing-up to the jury but for the making of an order under Part 7.'

31 Intermittent custody

Schedule 6 (intermittent custody) has effect.

PART 3 VICTIMS ETC

CHAPTER 1 THE VICTIMS' CODE

32 Code of practice for victims

(1) The Secretary of State must issue a code of practice as to the services to be provided to a victim of criminal conduct by persons appearing to him to have functions relating to –

(a) victims of criminal conduct, or
(b) any aspect of the criminal justice system.

(2) The code may restrict the application of its provisions to –

(a) specified descriptions of victims;
(b) victims of specified offences or descriptions of conduct;
(c) specified persons or descriptions of persons appearing to the Secretary of State to have functions of the kind mentioned in subsection (1).

(3) The code may include provision requiring or permitting the services which are to be provided to a victim to be provided to one or more others –

(a) instead of the victim (for example where the victim has died);
(b) as well as the victim.

(4) The code may make different provision for different purposes, including different provision for –

(a) different descriptions of victims;
(b) persons who have different functions or descriptions of functions;
(c) different areas.

(5) The code may not require anything to be done by –

(a) a person acting in a judicial capacity;
(b) a person acting in the discharge of a function of a member of the Crown Prosecution Service which involves the exercise of a discretion.

(6) In determining whether a person is a victim of criminal conduct for the purposes of this section, it is immaterial that no person has been charged with or convicted of an offence in respect of the conduct.

(7) In this section –

'criminal conduct' means conduct constituting an offence;
'specified' means specified in the code.

33 Procedure

(1) Subsections (2) to (7) apply in relation to a code of practice required to be issued under section 32.
(2) The Secretary of State must prepare a draft of the code.
(3) In preparing the draft the Secretary of State must consult the Attorney General and the Lord Chancellor.
(4) After preparing the draft the Secretary of State must –

(a) publish the draft;
(b) specify a period during which representations about the draft may be made to him.

(5) The Secretary of State must –

(a) consider in consultation with the Attorney General and the Lord Chancellor any representations made to him before the end of the specified period about the draft;
(b) if he thinks it appropriate, modify the draft in the light of any such representations.

(6) After the Secretary of State has proceeded under subsection (5) he must lay the code before Parliament.
(7) When he has laid the code before Parliament the Secretary of State must bring it into operation on such day as he appoints by order.
(8) The Secretary of State may from time to time revise a code previously brought into operation under this section; and subsections (2) to (7) apply to a revised code as they apply to the code as first prepared.
(9) But the Secretary of State may revise a code under subsection (8) only if it appears to him that the proposed revisions would not result in –
   (a) a significant reduction in the quality or extent of the services to be provided under the code, or
   (b) a significant restriction in the description of persons to whom services are to be provided under the code.

34 Effect of non-compliance

(1) If a person fails to perform a duty imposed on him by a code issued under section 32, the failure does not of itself make him liable to criminal or civil proceedings.
(2) But the code is admissible in evidence in criminal or civil proceedings and a court may take into account a failure to comply with the code in determining a question in the proceedings.

CHAPTER 2 REPRESENTATIONS AND INFORMATION

Imprisonment or detention

35 Victims' rights to make representations and receive information

(1) This section applies if –
   (a) a court convicts a person ('the offender') of a sexual or violent offence, and
   (b) a relevant sentence is imposed on him in respect of the offence.
(2) But section 39 applies (instead of this section) if a hospital direction and a limitation direction are given in relation to the offender.
(3) The local probation board for the area in which the sentence is imposed must take all reasonable steps to ascertain whether a person who appears to the board to be the victim of the offence or to act for the victim of the offence wishes –
   (a) to make representations about the matters specified in subsection (4);
   (b) to receive the information specified in subsection (5).
(4) The matters are –
   (a) whether the offender should be subject to any licence conditions or supervision requirements in the event of his release;
   (b) if so, what licence conditions or supervision requirements.
(5) The information is information about any licence conditions or supervision requirements to which the offender is to be subject in the event of his release.
(6) If a person whose wishes have been ascertained under subsection (3) makes representations to the local probation board mentioned in that subsection or the relevant local probation board about a matter specified in subsection (4), the relevant local probation board must forward those representations to the persons responsible for determining the matter.
(7) If a local probation board has ascertained under subsection (3) that a person wishes to receive the information specified in subsection (5), the relevant local probation board must take all reasonable steps –

(a) to inform the person whether or not the offender is to be subject to any licence conditions or supervision requirements in the event of his release,
(b) if he is, to provide the person with details of any licence conditions or supervision requirements which relate to contact with the victim or his family, and
(c) to provide the person with such other information as the relevant local probation board considers appropriate in all the circumstances of the case.

(8) The relevant local probation board is –

(a) in a case where the offender is to be supervised on release by an officer of a local probation board, that local probation board;
(b) in any other case, the local probation board for the area in which the prison or other place in which the offender is detained is situated.

Hospital orders

36 Victims' rights: preliminary

(1) This section applies if the conditions in subsections (2) and (3) are met.
(2) The first condition is that one of these applies in respect of a person ('the patient') charged with a sexual or violent offence –

(a) the patient is convicted of the offence;
(b) a verdict is returned that the patient is not guilty of the offence by reason of insanity;
(c) a finding is made –

(i) under section 4 of the Criminal Procedure (Insanity) Act 1964 (c. 84) that the patient is under a disability, and
(ii) under section 4A of that Act that he did the act or made the omission charged against him as the offence.

(3) The second condition is that a hospital order with a restriction order is made in respect of the patient by a court dealing with him for the offence.
(4) The local probation board for the area in which the determination mentioned in subsection (2)(a), (b) or (c) is made must take all reasonable steps to ascertain whether a person who appears to the board to be the victim of the offence or to act for the victim of the offence wishes –

(a) to make representations about the matters specified in subsection (5);
(b) to receive the information specified in subsection (6).

(5) The matters are –

(a) whether the patient should be subject to any conditions in the event of his discharge from hospital;
(b) if so, what conditions.

(6) The information is information about any conditions to which the patient is to be subject in the event of his discharge from hospital.

37 Representations

(1) This section applies if section 36 applies.
(2) If –

(a) a person makes representations about a matter specified in section 36(5) to the local probation board mentioned in section 36(4) or the relevant local probation board, and
(b) it appears to the relevant local probation board that the person is the victim of the offence or acts for the victim of the offence,

the relevant local probation board must forward the representations to the persons responsible for determining the matter.

(3) The duty in subsection (2) applies only while the restriction order made in respect of the patient is in force.

(4) The Secretary of State must inform the relevant local probation board if he is considering –

(a) whether to give a direction in respect of the patient under section 42(1) of the Mental Health Act 1983 (c. 20) (directions lifting restrictions),

(b) whether to discharge the patient under section 42(2) of that Act, either absolutely or subject to conditions, or

(c) if the patient has been discharged subject to conditions, whether to vary the conditions.

(5) A Mental Health Review Tribunal must inform the relevant local probation board if –

(a) an application is made to the tribunal by the patient under section 69, 70 or 75 of the Mental Health Act 1983 (applications concerning restricted patients), or

(b) the Secretary of State refers the patient's case to the tribunal under section 71 of that Act (references concerning restricted patients).

(6) Subsection (7) applies if –

(a) the relevant local probation board receives information under subsection (4) or (5), and

(b) a person who appears to the relevant local probation board to be the victim of the offence or to act for the victim of the offence –

(i) when his wishes were ascertained under section 36(4), expressed a wish to make representations about a matter specified in section 36(5), or

(ii) has made representations about such a matter to the relevant local probation board or the local probation board mentioned in section 36(4).

(7) The relevant local probation board must provide the information to the person.

(8) The relevant local probation board is –

(a) if the patient is to be discharged subject to a condition that he reside in a particular area, the local probation board for the area;

(b) in any other case, the local probation board for the area in which the hospital in which the patient is detained is situated.

38 Information

(1) This section applies if section 36 applies.

(2) Subsection (3) applies if a person who appears to the relevant local probation board to be the victim of the offence or to act for the victim of the offence –

(a) when his wishes were ascertained under section 36(4), expressed a wish to receive the information specified in section 36(6), or

(b) has subsequently informed the relevant local probation board that he wishes to receive that information.

(3) The relevant local probation board must take all reasonable steps –

(a) to inform that person whether or not the patient is to be subject to any conditions in the event of his discharge;

(b) if he is, to provide that person with details of any conditions which relate to contact with the victim or his family;

(c) if the restriction order in respect of the patient is to cease to have effect, to notify that person of the date on which it is to cease to have effect;

(d) to provide that person with such other information as the board considers appropriate in all the circumstances of the case.

(4) The Secretary of State must inform the relevant local probation board –
  (a) whether the patient is to be discharged;
  (b) if he is, whether he is to be discharged absolutely or subject to conditions;
  (c) if he is to be discharged subject to conditions, what the conditions are to be;
  (d) if he has been discharged subject to conditions –
    (i) of any variation of the conditions by the Secretary of State;
    (ii) of any recall to hospital under section 42(3) of the Mental Health Act 1983 (c. 20);
  (e) if the restriction order is to cease to have effect by virtue of action to be taken by the Secretary of State, of the date on which the restriction order is to cease to have effect.

(5) Subsections (6) and (7) apply (instead of subsection (4)) if –
  (a) an application is made to a Mental Health Review Tribunal by the patient under section 69, 70 or 75 of the Mental Health Act 1983 (c. 20) (applications concerning restricted patients), or
  (b) the Secretary of State refers the patient's case to a Mental Health Review Tribunal under section 71 of that Act (references concerning restricted patients).

(6) The tribunal must inform the relevant local probation board –
  (a) of the matters specified in subsection (4)(a) to (c);
  (b) if the patient has been discharged subject to conditions, of any variation of the conditions by the tribunal;
  (c) if the restriction order is to cease to have effect by virtue of action to be taken by the tribunal, of the date on which the restriction order is to cease to have effect.

(7) The Secretary of State must inform the relevant local probation board of the matters specified in subsection (4)(d) and (e).

(8) The duties in subsections (3) to (7) apply only while the restriction order is in force.

(9) The relevant local probation board has the meaning given in section 37(8).

Hospital directions

39 Victims' rights: preliminary

(1) This section applies if –
  (a) a person ('the offender') is convicted of a sexual or violent offence,
  (b) a relevant sentence is imposed on him in respect of the offence, and
  (c) a hospital direction and a limitation direction are given in relation to him by a court dealing with him for the offence.

(2) The local probation board for the area in which the hoşpital direction is given must take all reasonable steps to ascertain whether a person who appears to the board to be the victim of the offence or to act for the victim of the offence wishes –
  (a) to make representations about the matters specified in subsection (3);
  (b) to receive the information specified in subsection (4).

(3) The matters are –
  (a) whether the offender should, in the event of his discharge from hospital, be subject to any conditions and, if so, what conditions;
  (b) whether the offender should, in the event of his release from hospital, be subject to any licence conditions or supervision requirements and, if so, what licence conditions or supervision requirements;
  (c) if the offender is transferred to a prison or other institution in which he might have been detained if he had not been removed to hospital, whether he should, in the event of his release from prison or another such institution, be subject to

any licence conditions or supervision requirements and, if so, what licence conditions or supervision requirements.

(4) The information is –

(a) information about any conditions to which the offender is to be subject in the event of his discharge;

(b) information about any licence conditions or supervision requirements to which the offender is to be subject in the event of his release.

40 Representations

(1) This section applies if section 39 applies.

(2) If –

(a) a person makes representations about a matter specified in section 39(3) to the local probation board mentioned in section 39(2) or the relevant local probation board, and

(b) it appears to the relevant local probation board that the person is the victim of the offence or acts for the victim of the offence,

the relevant local probation board must forward the representations to the persons responsible for determining the matter.

(3) If the representations are about a matter specified in section 39(3)(a), the duty in subsection (2) applies only while the limitation direction given in relation to the offender is in force.

(4) The Secretary of State must inform the relevant local probation board if he is considering –

(a) whether to give a direction in respect of the offender under section 42(1) of the Mental Health Act 1983 (c. 20) (directions lifting restrictions),

(b) whether to discharge the offender under section 42(2) of that Act, either absolutely or subject to conditions, or

(c) if the offender has been discharged subject to conditions, whether to vary the conditions.

(5) A Mental Health Review Tribunal must inform the relevant local probation board if –

(a) an application is made to the tribunal by the offender under section 69, 70 or 75 of the Mental Health Act 1983 (applications concerning restricted patients), or

(b) the Secretary of State refers the offender's case to the tribunal under section 71 of that Act (references concerning restricted patients).

(6) Subsection (7) applies if –

(a) the relevant local probation board receives information under subsection (4) or (5), and

(b) a person who appears to the relevant local probation board to be the victim of the offence or to act for the victim of the offence –

(i) when his wishes were ascertained under section 39(2), expressed a wish to make representations about a matter specified in section 39(3)(a), or

(ii) has made representations about such a matter to the relevant local probation board or the local probation board mentioned in section 39(2).

(7) The relevant local probation board must provide the information to the person.

(8) The relevant local probation board is –

(a) if the offender is to be discharged from hospital subject to a condition that he reside in a particular area, the local probation board for the area;

(b) if the offender is to be supervised on release by an officer of a local probation board, that local probation board;

(c) in any other case, the local probation board for the area in which the hospital, prison or other place in which the offender is detained is situated.

41 Information

(1) This section applies if section 39 applies.

(2) Subsection (3) applies if a person who appears to the relevant local probation board to be the victim of the offence or to act for the victim of the offence –

(a) when his wishes were ascertained under section 39(2), expressed a wish to receive the information specified in section 39(4), or

(b) has subsequently informed the relevant local probation board that he wishes to receive that information.

(3) The relevant local probation board must take all reasonable steps –

(a) to inform that person whether or not the offender is to be subject to any conditions in the event of his discharge;

(b) if he is, to provide that person with details of any conditions which relate to contact with the victim or his family;

(c) if the limitation direction in respect of the offender is to cease to have effect, to notify that person of the date on which it is to cease to have effect;

(d) to inform that person whether or not the offender is to be subject to any licence conditions or supervision requirements in the event of his release;

(e) if he is, to provide that person with details of any licence conditions or supervision requirements which relate to contact with the victim or his family;

(f) to provide that person with such other information as the board considers appropriate in all the circumstances of the case.

(4) The Secretary of State must inform the relevant local probation board –

(a) whether the offender is to be discharged;

(b) if he is, whether he is to be discharged absolutely or subject to conditions;

(c) if he is to be discharged subject to conditions, what the conditions are to be;

(d) if he has been discharged subject to conditions –

(i) of any variation of the conditions by the Secretary of State;

(ii) of any recall to hospital under section 42(3) of the Mental Health Act 1983 (c. 20);

(e) if the limitation direction is to cease to have effect by virtue of action to be taken by the Secretary of State, of the date on which the limitation direction is to cease to have effect.

(5) Subsections (6) and (7) apply (instead of subsection (4)) if –

(a) an application is made to a Mental Health Review Tribunal by the offender under section 69, 70 or 75 of the Mental Health Act 1983 (c. 20) (applications concerning restricted patients), or

(b) the Secretary of State refers the offender's case to a Mental Health Review Tribunal under section 71 of that Act (references concerning restricted patients).

(6) The tribunal must inform the relevant local probation board –

(a) of the matters specified in subsection (4)(a) to (c);

(b) if the offender has been discharged subject to conditions, of any variation of the conditions by the tribunal;

(c) if the limitation direction is to cease to have effect by virtue of action to be taken by the tribunal, of the date on which the limitation direction is to cease to have effect.

(7) The Secretary of State must inform the relevant local probation board of the matters specified in subsection (4)(d) and (e).

(8) The duties in subsections (3)(a) to (c) and (4) to (7) apply only while the limitation direction is in force.

(9) The relevant local probation board has the meaning given in section 40(8).

Transfer directions

42 Victims' rights: preliminary

(1) This section applies if –

(a) a person ('the offender') is convicted of a sexual or violent offence,
(b) a relevant sentence is imposed on him in respect of the offence, and
(c) while the offender is serving the sentence, the Secretary of State gives a transfer direction and a restriction direction in respect of him.

(2) The local probation board for the area in which the hospital specified in the transfer direction is situated must take all reasonable steps to ascertain whether a person who appears to the board to be the victim of the offence or to act for the victim of the offence wishes –

(a) to make representations about the matters specified in subsection (3);
(b) to receive the information specified in subsection (4).

(3) The matters are –

(a) whether the offender should be subject to any conditions in the event of his discharge from hospital;
(b) if so, what conditions.

(4) The information is information about any conditions to which the offender is to be subject in the event of his discharge from hospital.

43 Representations

(1) This section applies if section 42 applies.
(2) If –

(a) a person makes representations about a matter specified in section 42(3) to the local probation board mentioned in section 42(2) or the relevant local probation board, and
(b) it appears to the relevant local probation board that the person is the victim of the offence or acts for the victim of the offence,

the relevant local probation board must forward the representations to the persons responsible for determining the matter.

(3) The duty in subsection (2) applies only while the restriction direction given in respect of the offender is in force.
(4) The Secretary of State must inform the relevant local probation board if he is considering –

(a) whether to give a direction in respect of the offender under section 42(1) of the Mental Health Act 1983 (c. 20) (directions lifting restrictions),
(b) whether to discharge the offender under section 42(2) of that Act, either absolutely or subject to conditions, or
(c) if the offender has been discharged subject to conditions, whether to vary the conditions.

(5) A Mental Health Review Tribunal must inform the relevant local probation board if –

(a) an application is made to the tribunal by the offender under section 69, 70 or 75 of the Mental Health Act 1983 (applications concerning restricted patients), or
(b) the Secretary of State refers the offender's case to the tribunal under section 71 of that Act (references concerning restricted patients).

(6) Subsection (7) applies if –

(a) the relevant local probation board receives information under subsection (4) or (5), and
(b) a person who appears to the relevant local probation board to be the victim of the offence or to act for the victim of the offence –

(i) when his wishes were ascertained under section 42(2), expressed a wish to make representations about a matter specified in section 42(3), or

(ii) has made representations about such a matter to the relevant local probation board or the local probation board mentioned in section 42(2).

(7) The relevant local probation board must provide the information to the person.

(8) The relevant local probation board is –

(a) if the offender is to be discharged subject to a condition that he reside in a particular area, the local probation board for the area;

(b) in any other case, the local probation board for the area in which the hospital in which the offender is detained is situated.

44 Information

(1) This section applies if section 42 applies.

(2) Subsection (3) applies if a person who appears to the relevant local probation board to be the victim of the offence or to act for the victim of the offence –

(a) when his wishes were ascertained under section 42(2), expressed a wish to receive the information specified in section 42(4), or

(b) has subsequently informed the relevant local probation board that he wishes to receive that information.

(3) The relevant local probation board must take all reasonable steps –

(a) to inform that person whether or not the offender is to be subject to any conditions in the event of his discharge;

(b) if he is, to provide that person with details of any conditions which relate to contact with the victim or his family;

(c) if the restriction direction in respect of the offender is to cease to have effect, to notify that person of the date on which it is to cease to have effect;

(d) to provide that person with such other information as the board considers appropriate in all the circumstances of the case.

(4) The Secretary of State must inform the relevant local probation board –

(a) whether the offender is to be discharged;

(b) if he is, whether he is to be discharged absolutely or subject to conditions;

(c) if he is to be discharged subject to conditions, what the conditions are to be;

(d) if he has been discharged subject to conditions –

(i) of any variation of the conditions by the Secretary of State;

(ii) of any recall to hospital under section 42(3) of the Mental Health Act 1983 (c. 20);

(e) if the restriction direction is to cease to have effect by virtue of action to be taken by the Secretary of State, of the date on which the restriction direction is to cease to have effect.

(5) Subsections (6) and (7) apply (instead of subsection (4)) if –

(a) an application is made to a Mental Health Review Tribunal by the offender under section 69, 70 or 75 of the Mental Health Act 1983 (applications concerning restricted patients), or

(b) the Secretary of State refers the offender's case to a Mental Health Review Tribunal under section 71 of that Act (references concerning restricted patients).

(6) The tribunal must inform the relevant local probation board –

(a) of the matters specified in subsection (4)(a) to (c);

(b) if the offender has been discharged subject to conditions, of any variation of the conditions by the tribunal;

(c) if the restriction direction is to cease to have effect by virtue of action to be taken by the tribunal, of the date on which the restriction direction is to cease to have effect.

(7) The Secretary of State must inform the relevant local probation board of the matters specified in subsection (4)(d) and (e).
(8) The duties in subsections (3) to (7) apply only while the restriction direction is in force.
(9) The relevant local probation board has the meaning given in section 43(8).

Interpretation

45 Interpretation: sections 35 to 44

(1) In sections 35 to 44 –

'court' does not include a court-martial or the Courts-Martial Appeal Court;
'hospital direction' has the meaning given in section 45A(3)(a) of the Mental Health Act 1983 (c. 20);
'hospital order' has the meaning given in section 37(4) of that Act;
'licence condition' means a condition in a licence;
'limitation direction' has the meaning given in section 45A(3)(b) of the Mental Health Act 1983;
'local probation board' means a local probation board established under section 4 of the Criminal Justice and Court Services Act 2000 (c. 43);
'relevant sentence' means any of these –

(a) a sentence of imprisonment for a term of 12 months or more;
(b) a sentence of detention during Her Majesty's pleasure;
(c) a sentence of detention for a period of 12 months or more under section 91 of the Powers of Criminal Courts (Sentencing) Act 2000 (c. 6) (offenders under 18 convicted of certain serious offences);
(d) a detention and training order for a term of 12 months or more;

'restriction direction' has the meaning given in section 49(2) of the Mental Health Act 1983;
'restriction order' has the meaning given in section 41(1) of that Act;
'supervision requirements' means requirements specified in a notice under section 103(6) of the Powers of Criminal Courts (Sentencing) Act 2000;
'transfer direction' has the meaning given in section 47(1) of the Mental Health Act 1983.

(2) For the purposes of sections 35 to 44, an offence is a sexual or violent offence if it is any of these –

(a) murder or an offence specified in Schedule 15 to the Criminal Justice Act 2003 (c. 44);
(b) an offence in respect of which the patient or offender is subject to the notification requirements of Part 2 of the Sexual Offences Act 2003 (c. 42));
(c) an offence against a child within the meaning of Part 2 of the Criminal Justice and Court Services Act 2000.

Northern Ireland

46 Victims of mentally disordered persons

(1) The Justice (Northern Ireland) Act 2002 (c. 26) is amended as follows.
(2) After section 69 (views on temporary release) insert –

'69A Information about discharge and leave of absence of mentally disordered persons

(1) The Secretary of State must make a scheme requiring the Secretary of State to make available to persons falling within subsection (2) information about –

(a) the discharge from hospital of, or
(b) the grant of leave of absence from hospital to,

persons in respect of whom relevant determinations have been made.

(2) The persons referred to in subsection (1) are victims of the offences in respect of which the determinations were made who wish to receive the information.

(3) A relevant determination is made in respect of a person if –

(a) a hospital order with a restriction order is made in respect of him by a court dealing with him for an offence, or
(b) a transfer direction and a restriction direction are given in respect of him while he is serving a sentence of imprisonment in respect of an offence.

(4) The Secretary of State may from time to time make a new scheme or alterations to a scheme.

(5) The information to be made available under a scheme must include information as to any relevant conditions to which a person in respect of whom a relevant determination has been made is to be subject in the event of –

(a) his discharge from hospital, or
(b) the grant of leave of absence from hospital to him.

(6) A condition is relevant for the purposes of subsection (5) if it appears to the Secretary of State that it might affect a victim of an offence in respect of which the determination was made.

(7) A scheme may require the Secretary of State to take all reasonable steps to ascertain whether a person who appears to him to be the victim of an offence in respect of which a relevant determination has been made wishes to make representations about the matters specified in subsection (8).

(8) The matters are –

(a) whether the person in respect of whom the determination has been made should be subject to any conditions in the event of his discharge from hospital or the grant of leave of absence from hospital to him;
(b) if so, what conditions.

(9) A scheme that includes provision such as is mentioned in subsection (7) must specify how the representations are to be made.

(10) A scheme may require other information in relation to the discharge of, or the grant of leave of absence to, persons in respect of whom relevant determinations are made to be made available under the scheme.

(11) The other information may include, in cases of a description specified by the scheme or in which the Secretary of State considers it appropriate, the date on which it is anticipated that a person in respect of whom a relevant determination has been made will be discharged or granted leave of absence from hospital.

(12) Subsections (5) to (8) of section 68 apply in relation to a scheme made under this section as they apply in relation to a scheme made under that section.

(13) A scheme may make different provision in relation to different descriptions of persons in respect of whom a relevant determination is made.

69B Views on leave of absence

(1) If a person who is the victim of an offence in respect of which a relevant determination has been made makes to the Secretary of State representations falling within subsection (2) the Secretary of State has the obligations specified in subsection (3).

(2) Representations fall within this subsection if they are to the effect that the grant of leave of absence to the person in respect of whom the determination has been made would threaten the safety, or otherwise adversely affect the well-being, of –

(a) the actual victim of the offence in respect of which the determination was made, or

(b) a person who is regarded for the purposes of a scheme under section 69A as a victim of that offence by virtue of section 68(5) (as applied by section 69A(12)).

(3) The Secretary of State must –

(a) have regard to the representations in deciding whether he should give his consent to leave of absence being granted, and

(b) inform the victim of any such decision.

(4) Section 69A(3) (relevant determination) applies for the purposes of this section.'

(3) In section 70 (supplementary), after subsection (3) insert –

'(4) In sections 68 and 69 references to a person serving a sentence of imprisonment in Northern Ireland include a person detained in hospital pursuant to a transfer direction and a restriction direction.

(5) In subsection (4) and section 69A(3) –

"restriction direction" has the meaning given in Article 55(2) of the Mental Health (Northern Ireland) Order 1986;

"transfer direction" has the meaning given in Article 53(2) of that Order.

(6) In section 69A(3) –

"hospital order" has the meaning given in Article 44(1) of the Mental Health (Northern Ireland) Order 1986;

"restriction order" has the meaning given in Article 47(1) of that Order;

"sentence of imprisonment" has the meaning given in Article 53(5) of that Order.

(7) In sections 69A and 69B "leave of absence" means leave of absence under Article 15 of the Mental Health (Northern Ireland) Order 1986.'

(4) In section 90(5) (statutory rules), in paragraph (b) after 'section 68' insert 'or 69A'.

CHAPTER 3 OTHER MATTERS RELATING TO VICTIMS ETC

Parliamentary Commissioner

47 Investigations by Parliamentary Commissioner

Schedule 7 (which amends the Parliamentary Commissioner Act 1967 (c. 13)) has effect.

Commissioner for Victims and Witnesses

48 Commissioner for Victims and Witnesses

(1) The Secretary of State must appoint a Commissioner for Victims and Witnesses (referred to in this Part as the Commissioner).

(2) Before appointing the Commissioner the Secretary of State must consult the Attorney General and the Lord Chancellor as to the person to be appointed.

(3) The Commissioner is a corporation sole.

(4) The Commissioner is not to be regarded –

(a) as the servant or agent of the Crown, or

(b) as enjoying any status, immunity or privilege of the Crown.

(5) The Commissioner's property is not to be regarded as property of, or held on behalf of, the Crown.
(6) Schedule 8 (which make further provision in connection with the Commissioner) has effect.

49 General functions of Commissioner

(1) The Commissioner must –
   (a) promote the interests of victims and witnesses;
   (b) take such steps as he considers appropriate with a view to encouraging good practice in the treatment of victims and witnesses;
   (c) keep under review the operation of the code of practice issued under section 32.
(2) The Commissioner may, for any purpose connected with the performance of his duties under subsection (1) –
   (a) make proposals to the Secretary of State for amending the code (at the request of the Secretary of State or on his own initiative);
   (b) make a report to the Secretary of State;
   (c) make recommendations to an authority within his remit;
   (d) undertake or arrange for or support (financially or otherwise) the carrying out of research;
   (e) consult any person he thinks appropriate.
(3) If the Commissioner makes a report to the Secretary of State under subsection (2)(b) –
   (a) the Commissioner must send a copy of the report to the Attorney General and the Lord Chancellor;
   (b) the Secretary of State must lay a copy of the report before Parliament and arrange for the report to be published.

50 Advice

(1) If he is required to do so by a Minister of the Crown, the Commissioner must give advice to the Minister of the Crown in connection with any matter which –
   (a) is specified by the Minister, and
   (b) relates to victims or witnesses.
(2) If he is required to do so by or on behalf of an authority within his remit, the Commissioner must give advice to the authority in connection with the information provided or to be provided by or on behalf of the authority to victims or witnesses.
(3) In this section 'Minister of the Crown' includes the Treasury.

51 Restrictions on exercise of functions

The Commissioner must not exercise any of his functions in relation to –
   (a) a particular victim or witness;
   (b) the bringing or conduct of particular proceedings;
   (c) anything done or omitted to be done by a person acting in a judicial capacity or on the instructions of or on behalf of such a person.

52 'Victims' and 'witnesses'

(1) This section applies for the purposes of sections 48 to 51.
(2) 'Victim' means –
   (a) a victim of an offence, or
   (b) a victim of anti-social behaviour.
(3) It is immaterial for the purposes of subsection (2)(a) that –
   (a) no complaint has been made about the offence;

(b) no person has been charged with or convicted of the offence.

(4) 'Witness' means a person (other than a defendant) –

(a) who has witnessed conduct in relation to which he may be or has been called to give evidence in relevant proceedings;
(b) who is able to provide or has provided anything which might be used or has been used as evidence in relevant proceedings; or
(c) who is able to provide or has provided anything mentioned in subsection (5) (whether or not admissible in evidence in relevant proceedings).

(5) The things referred to in subsection (4)(c) are –

(a) anything which might tend to confirm, has tended to confirm or might have tended to confirm evidence which may be, has been or could have been admitted in relevant proceedings;
(b) anything which might be, has been or might have been referred to in evidence given in relevant proceedings by another person;
(c) anything which might be, has been or might have been used as the basis for any cross examination in the course of relevant proceedings.

(6) For the purposes of subsection (4) –

(a) a person is a defendant in relation to any criminal proceedings if he might be, has been or might have been charged with or convicted of an offence in the proceedings;
(b) a person is a defendant in relation to any other relevant proceedings if he might be, has been or might have been the subject of an order made in those proceedings.

(7) In subsections (4) to (6) 'relevant proceedings' means –

(a) criminal proceedings;
(b) proceedings of any other kind in respect of anti-social behaviour.

(8) For the purposes of this section –

(a) 'anti-social behaviour' means behaviour by a person which causes or is likely to cause harassment, alarm or distress to one or more persons not of the same household as the person;
(b) a person is a victim of anti-social behaviour if the behaviour has caused him harassment, alarm or distress and he is not of the same household as the person who engages in the behaviour.

53 Authorities within Commissioner's remit

(1) For the purposes of this Part the authorities within the Commissioner's remit are those specified in Schedule 9.
(2) An authority specified in Schedule 9 that has functions in relation to an area outside England and Wales is within the Commissioner's remit only to the extent that it discharges its functions in relation to England and Wales.
(3) Subsection (2) does not apply in relation to the Foreign and Commonwealth Office.
(4) The Secretary of State may by order amend Schedule 9 by –

(a) adding an authority appearing to him to exercise functions of a public nature;
(b) omitting an authority;
(c) changing the description of an authority.

(5) In preparing a draft of an order under subsection (4) the Secretary of State must consult the Attorney General and the Lord Chancellor.

Disclosure of information

54 Disclosure of information

(1) A person may disclose information to a relevant authority for a purpose specified in subsection (2).
(2) The purposes are purposes connected with any of these –

(a) compliance with the code issued under section 32;
(b) compliance with sections 35 to 44;
(c) the carrying out of the functions of the Commissioner.

(3) These are relevant authorities –

(a) a person required to do anything under the code issued under section 32;
(b) a local probation board established under section 4 of the Criminal Justice and Court Services Act 2000 (c. 43);
(c) the Commissioner;
(d) an authority within the Commissioner's remit.

(4) The Secretary of State may by order –

(a) amend subsection (2) by adding any purpose appearing to him to be connected with the assistance of victims of offences or anti-social behaviour, witnesses of offences or anti-social behaviour or other persons affected by offences or anti-social behaviour;
(b) amend subsection (3) by adding any authority appearing to him to exercise functions of a public nature.

(5) The reference in subsection (4)(a) to persons affected by offences does not include persons accused or convicted of offences.
(6) The Secretary of State may exercise the power in subsection (4) only after consulting the Attorney General and the Lord Chancellor.
(7) Nothing in this section authorises the making of a disclosure which contravenes the Data Protection Act 1998 (c. 29).
(8) This section does not affect a power to disclose which exists apart from this section.

Victims' Advisory Panel

55 Victims' Advisory Panel

(1) The Secretary of State must appoint persons to form a panel, to be known as the Victims' Advisory Panel.
(2) The Secretary of State must consult the Attorney General and the Lord Chancellor before –

(a) appointing a person to the Panel, or
(b) removing a person from the Panel.

(3) The Secretary of State must consult the Panel at such times and in such manner as he thinks appropriate on matters appearing to him to relate to victims of offences or anti-social behaviour or witnesses of offences or anti-social behaviour.
(4) The Secretary of State may reimburse the members of the Panel for such of their travelling and other expenses as he thinks appropriate.
(5) If the Secretary of State consults the Panel under subsection (3) in a particular year, he must arrange for the Panel to prepare a report for the year –

(a) summarising what the Panel has done in response to the consultation, and
(b) dealing with such other matters as the Panel consider appropriate.

(6) If a report is prepared under subsection (5), the Secretary of State must –

(a) arrange for it to be published, and
(b) lay it before Parliament.

(7) The non-statutory Victims' Advisory Panel is to be treated as having been established in accordance with this section.
(8) If the Secretary of State consults the non-statutory Victims' Advisory Panel on a matter mentioned in subsection (3) before the date on which this section comes into force, the consultation is to be treated as taking place under subsection (3).
(9) The non-statutory Victims' Advisory Panel is the unincorporated body of persons known as the Victims' Advisory Panel established by the Secretary of State before the date on which this section comes into force.
(10) In this section 'year' means a period of 12 months beginning on 1 April.

Grants

56 Grants for assisting victims, witnesses etc

(1) The Secretary of State may pay such grants to such persons as he considers appropriate in connection with measures which appear to him to be intended to assist victims, witnesses or other persons affected by offences.
(2) The Secretary of State may make a grant under this section subject to such conditions as he considers appropriate.

Criminal injuries compensation

57 Recovery of criminal injuries compensation from offenders

(1) The Criminal Injuries Compensation Act 1995 (c. 53) is amended as follows.
(2) After section 7 insert –

> **'7A Recovery of compensation from offenders: general**
>
> (1) The Secretary of State may, by regulations made by statutory instrument, make provision for the recovery from an appropriate person of an amount equal to all or part of the compensation paid in respect of a criminal injury.
> (2) An appropriate person is a person who has been convicted of an offence in respect of the criminal injury.
> (3) The amount recoverable from a person under the regulations must be determined by reference only to the extent to which the criminal injury is directly attributable to an offence of which he has been convicted.
> (4) The regulations may confer functions in respect of recovery on –
>
> (a) claims officers;
> (b) if a Scheme manager has been appointed, persons appointed by the Scheme manager under section 3(4)(a).
>
> (5) The regulations may not authorise the recovery of an amount in respect of compensation from a person to the extent that the compensation has been repaid in accordance with the Scheme.
>
> **7B Recovery notices**
>
> (1) If, under regulations made under section 7A(1), an amount has been determined as recoverable from a person, he must be given a notice (a "recovery notice") in accordance with the regulations which –
>
> (a) requires him to pay that amount, and
> (b) contains the information mentioned in subsection (2).
>
> (2) The information is –
>
> (a) the reasons for the determination that an amount is recoverable from the person;

(b) the basis on which the amount has been determined;
(c) the way in which and the date before which the amount is required to be paid;
(d) the means by which the amount may be recovered if it is not paid in accordance with the notice;
(e) the grounds on which and the procedure by means of which he may seek a review if he objects to –
(i) the determination that an amount is recoverable from him;
(ii) the amount determined as recoverable from him.

(3) The Secretary of State may by order made by statutory instrument amend subsection (2) by –
(a) adding information;
(b) omitting information;
(c) changing the description of information.

7C Review of recovery determinations

(1) Regulations under section 7A(1) shall include provision for the review, in such circumstances as may be prescribed by the regulations, of –
(a) a determination that an amount is recoverable from a person;
(b) the amount determined as recoverable from a person.

(2) A person from whom an amount has been determined as recoverable under the regulations may seek such a review only on the grounds –
(a) that he has not been convicted of an offence to which the injury is directly attributable;
(b) that the compensation paid was not determined in accordance with the Scheme;
(c) that the amount determined as recoverable from him was not determined in accordance with the regulations.

(3) Any such review must be conducted by a person other than the person who made the determination under review.

(4) The person conducting any such review may –
(a) set aside the determination that the amount is recoverable;
(b) reduce the amount determined as recoverable;
(c) increase the amount determined as recoverable;
(d) determine to take no action under paragraphs (a) to (c).

(5) But the person conducting any such review may increase the amount determined as recoverable if (but only if) it appears to that person that the interests of justice require the amount to be increased.

7D Recovery proceedings

(1) An amount determined as recoverable from a person under regulations under section 7A(1) is recoverable from him as a debt due to the Crown if (but only if) –
(a) he has been given a recovery notice in accordance with the regulations which complies with the requirements of section 7B, and
(b) he has failed to pay the amount in accordance with the notice.

(2) In any proceedings for the recovery of the amount from a person, it is a defence for the person to show –
(a) that he has not been convicted of an offence to which the injury is directly attributable;

(b) that the compensation paid was not determined in accordance with the Scheme; or
(c) that the amount determined as recoverable from him was not determined in accordance with regulations under section 7A.

(3) In any such proceedings, except for the purposes of subsection (2)(b), no question may be raised or finding made as to the amount that was, or ought to have been, the subject of an award.

(4) For the purposes of section 9 of the Limitation Act 1980 (time limit for actions for sums recoverable by statute to run from date on which cause of action accrued) the cause of action to recover that amount shall be taken to have accrued –

(a) on the date on which the compensation was paid; or
(b) if later, on the date on which a person from whom an amount is sought to be recovered was convicted of an offence to which the injury is directly attributable.

(5) If that person is convicted of more than one such offence and the convictions are made on different dates, the reference in subsection (4)(b) to the date on which he was convicted of such an offence shall be taken to be a reference to the earlier or earliest (as the case may be) of the dates on which he was convicted of such an offence.'.

(3) In section 9(7) (financial provisions: sums payable into Consolidated Fund), after 'section 3(1)(c)' insert ', or by virtue of regulations made under section 7A(1),'.

(4) In section 11, after subsection (8) insert –

'(8A) No regulations under section 7A(1) or order under section 7B(3) shall be made unless a draft of the regulations or order has been laid before Parliament and approved by a resolution of each House.'

PART 4 SUPPLEMENTARY

58 Amendments and repeals

(1) Schedule 10 (minor and consequential amendments) has effect.
(2) The provisions mentioned in Schedule 11 are repealed or revoked to the extent specified.

59 Transitional and transitory provisions

Schedule 12 (transitional and transitory provisions) has effect.

60 Commencement

The preceding provisions of this Act come into force in accordance with provision made by the Secretary of State by order.

61 Orders

(1) An order under this Act –

(a) may make different provision for different purposes;
(b) may include supplementary, incidental, saving or transitional provisions.

(2) Any power to make an order under this Act is exercisable by statutory instrument.
(3) A statutory instrument containing an order under section 9(6) or 33(7) is subject to annulment in pursuance of a resolution of either House of Parliament.
(4) No order may be made under section 14(5), 53(4) or 54(4) unless a draft of the order has been laid before Parliament and approved by a resolution of each House.

62 Extent

(1) Subject to the following provisions of this section, Parts 1 to 3 extend to England and Wales only.

(2) The following provisions extend also to Northern Ireland –
section 5;
section 9;
sections 17 to 21;
Schedule 1;
section 56;

(3) The following provisions extend to Northern Ireland only –
section 7;
section 10(2);
section 13;
section 23;
section 46.

(4) Section 8, so far as relating to proceedings before courts-martial constituted under a particular Act mentioned in subsection (2) of that section, has the same extent as that Act.

(5) An amendment, repeal or revocation in Schedule 3, 7, 8, 10 or 11 has the same extent as the provision to which it relates.

63 Short title

This Act may be cited as the Domestic Violence, Crime and Victims Act 2004.

SCHEDULES

SCHEDULE 1 MODIFICATION OF SECTIONS 17 TO 20 FOR NORTHERN IRELAND

Section 21

1 For section 18 substitute –

'18 Procedure for applications under section 17

(1) An application under section 17 must be determined –

(a) at a preparatory hearing (within the meaning of the 1988 Order), or
(b) at a hearing specified in, or for which provision is made by, Crown Court rules.

(2) The parties to a hearing mentioned in subsection (1) at which an application under section 17 is to be determined must be given an opportunity to make representations with respect to the application.
(3) Article 6(1) of the 1988 Order (which sets out the purposes of preparatory hearings) is to have effect as if the purposes there mentioned included the purpose of determining an application under section 17.
(4) Article 8(11) of the 1988 Order (appeal to Court of Appeal) is to have effect as if it also provided for an appeal to the Court of Appeal to lie from the determination by a judge of an application under section 17.
(5) In this section "the 1988 Order" means the Criminal Justice (Serious Fraud) (Northern Ireland) Order 1988.

18A Appeals in respect of hearings under section 18(1)(b)

(1) An appeal shall lie to the Court of Appeal from the refusal by a judge at a hearing mentioned in section 18(1)(b) of an application under section 17 or from an order of a judge at such a hearing under section 17(2) which is made on the determination of such an application.
(2) Such an appeal may be brought only with the leave of the judge or the Court of Appeal.
(3) An order or a refusal of an application from which an appeal under this section lies is not to take effect –

(a) before the expiration of the period for bringing an appeal under this section, or
(b) if such an appeal is brought, before the appeal is finally disposed of or abandoned.

(4) On the termination of the hearing of an appeal under this section, the Court of Appeal may –

(a) where the appeal is from an order, confirm or revoke the order, or
(b) where the appeal is from a refusal of an application, confirm the refusal or make the order which is the subject of the application.

(5) In section 31(1) of the Criminal Appeal (Northern Ireland) Act 1980 (right of appeal to House of Lords) for "Act or" substitute "Act, section 18A of the Domestic Violence, Crime and Victims Act 2004,".
(6) In section 35 of that Act (bail) after "appeal under" insert "section 18A of the Domestic Violence, Crime and Victims Act 2004,".
(7) The Secretary of State may make an order containing provision, in relation to proceedings before the Court of Appeal under this section, which corresponds to any provision, in relation to appeals or other proceedings before

that court, which is contained in the Criminal Appeal (Northern Ireland) Act 1980 (subject to any specified modifications).

(8) A statutory instrument containing an order under subsection (7) is subject to annulment in pursuance of a resolution of either House of Parliament.

18B Reporting restrictions

(1) Sections 41 and 42 of the Criminal Procedure and Investigations Act 1996 are to apply in relation to –

(a) a hearing of the kind mentioned in section 18(1)(b), and

(b) any appeal or application for leave to appeal relating to such a hearing,

as they apply in relation to a ruling under section 40 of that Act, but subject to the following modifications.

(2) Section 41(2) of that Act is to have effect as if for paragraphs (a) to (d) there were substituted –

"(a) a hearing of the kind mentioned in section 18(1)(b) of the Domestic Violence, Crime and Victims Act 2004;

(b) any appeal or application for leave to appeal relating to such a hearing."

(3) Section 41(3) of that Act is to have effect as if –

(a) for "(2)" there were substituted "(2)(a) or an application to that judge for leave to appeal to the Court of Appeal", and

(b) after "matter", in the second place where it occurs, there were inserted "or application".

(4) Section 41 of that Act is to have effect as if after subsection (3) there were inserted –

"(3A) The Court of Appeal may order that subsection (1) shall not apply, or shall not apply to a specified extent, to a report of –

(a) an appeal to that Court, or

(b) an application to that Court for leave to appeal.

(3B) The House of Lords may order that subsection (1) shall not apply, or shall not apply to a specified extent, to a report of –

(a) an appeal to that House, or

(b) an application to that House for leave to appeal."

(5) Section 41(4) of that Act is to have effect as if for "(3) the judge" there were substituted "(3), (3A) or (3B), the judge, the Court of Appeal or the House of Lords".

(6) Section 41(5) of that Act is to have effect as if for "(3) the judge" there were substituted "(3), (3A) or (3B), the judge, the Court of Appeal or the House of Lords".'

2 In section 19(3) after 'enactment' insert '(including any provision of Northern Ireland legislation)'.

3 In section 19(4)(b) for the words from 'section' to 'etc)' substitute 'section 16(1) of the Criminal Appeal (Northern Ireland) Act 1980 (notice of appeal or application for leave)'.

4 In section 19(5) for 'section 18(2) of the Criminal Appeal Act 1968' substitute 'section 16(1) of the Criminal Appeal (Northern Ireland) Act 1980'.

5 For section 19(7) substitute –

'(7) Nothing in this section or section 17, 18, 18A, 18B or 20 affects the requirement under Article 49A of the Mental Health (Northern Ireland) Order 1986 that any question, finding or verdict mentioned in that Article be determined, made or returned by a jury.'

6 For section 20(2) substitute –

'(2) Without limiting subsection (1), rules of court may in particular make provision –

(a) for time limits within which applications under section 17 must be made or within which other things in connection with that section or sections 18 to 19 must be done;

(b) in relation to hearings of the kind mentioned in section 18(1)(b).'

7 In section 20(3) –

(a) after 'section' insert 'or section 18(1)(b)';

(b) after 'enactment' insert '(including any provision of Northern Ireland legislation)'.

SCHEDULE 2 SUPERVISION ORDERS ON FINDING OF INSANITY OR UNFITNESS TO PLEAD ETC

Section 24

The following is the Schedule inserted before Schedule 2 to the Criminal Procedure (Insanity) Act 1964 (c. 84) –

'SCHEDULE 1A SUPERVISION ORDERS

Section 5A

PART 1

PRELIMINARY

1 (1) In this Schedule "supervision order" means an order which requires the person in respect of whom it is made ("the supervised person") to be under the supervision of a social worker or an officer of a local probation board ("the supervising officer") for a period specified in the order of not more than two years.

(2) A supervision order may, in accordance with paragraph 4 or 5 below, require the supervised person to submit, during the whole of that period or such part of it as may be specified in the order, to treatment by or under the direction of a registered medical practitioner.

(3) The Secretary of State may by order direct that sub-paragraph (1) above shall be amended by substituting, for the period for the time being specified there, such period as may be specified in the order.

(4) An order under sub-paragraph (3) above may make in paragraph 11(2) below any amendment which the Secretary of State thinks necessary in consequence of any substitution made by the order.

(5) The power of the Secretary of State to make orders under sub-paragraph (3) above shall be exercisable by statutory instrument which shall be subject to annulment in pursuance of a resolution of either House of Parliament.

PART 2

MAKING AND EFFECT OF ORDERS

Circumstances in which orders may be made

2 (1) The court shall not make a supervision order unless it is satisfied that, having regard to all the circumstances of the case, the making of such an order is the most suitable means of dealing with the accused or appellant.

(2) The court shall not make a supervision order unless it is also satisfied –

(a) that the supervising officer intended to be specified in the order is willing to undertake the supervision; and

(b) that arrangements have been made for the treatment intended to be specified in the order.

Making of orders and general requirements

3 (1) A supervision order shall either –

(a) specify the local social services authority area in which the supervised person resides or will reside, and require him to be under the supervision of a social worker of the local social services authority for that area; or

(b) specify the local justice area in which that person resides or will reside, and require him to be under the supervision of an officer of a local probation board appointed for or assigned to that area.

(2) Before making such an order, the court shall explain to the supervised person in ordinary language –

(a) the effect of the order (including any requirements proposed to be included in the order in accordance with paragraph 4, 5 or 8 below); and

(b) that a magistrates' court has power under paragraphs 9 to 11 below to review the order on the application either of the supervised person or of the supervising officer.

(3) After making such an order, the court shall forthwith give copies of the order to an officer of a local probation board assigned to the court, and he shall give a copy –

(a) to the supervised person; and

(b) to the supervising officer.

(4) After making such an order, the court shall also send to the designated officer for the local justice area in which the supervised person resides or will reside ("the local justice area concerned") –

(a) a copy of the order; and

(b) such documents and information relating to the case as it considers likely to be of assistance to a court acting for that area in the exercise of its functions in relation to the order.

(5) Where such an order is made, the supervised person shall keep in touch with the supervising officer in accordance with such instructions as he may from time to time be given by that officer and shall notify him of any change of address.

Requirements as to medical treatment

4 (1) A supervision order may, if the court is satisfied as mentioned in sub-paragraph (2) below, include a requirement that the supervised person shall submit, during the whole of the period specified in the order or during such part of that period as may be so specified, to treatment by or under the direction of a registered medical practitioner with a view to the improvement of his mental condition.

(2) The court may impose such a requirement only if satisfied on the written or oral evidence of two or more registered medical practitioners, at least one of whom is duly registered, that the mental condition of the supervised person –

(a) is such as requires and may be susceptible to treatment; but
(b) is not such as to warrant the making of a hospital order within the meaning of the Mental Health Act 1983.

(3) The treatment required under this paragraph by any such order shall be such one of the following kinds of treatment as may be specified in the order, that is to say –

(a) treatment as a non-resident patient at such institution or place as may be specified in the order; and
(b) treatment by or under the direction of such registered medical practitioner as may be so specified;

but the nature of the treatment shall not be specified in the order except as mentioned in paragraph (a) or (b) above.

5 (1) This paragraph applies where the court is satisfied on the written or oral evidence of two or more registered medical practitioners that –

(a) because of his medical condition, other than his mental condition, the supervised person is likely to pose a risk to himself or others; and
(b) the condition may be susceptible to treatment.

(2) The supervision order may (whether or not it includes a requirement under paragraph 4 above) include a requirement that the supervised person shall submit, during the whole of the period specified in the order or during such part of that period as may be so specified, to treatment by or under the direction of a registered medical practitioner with a view to the improvement of the condition.

(3) The treatment required under this paragraph by any such order shall be such one of the following kinds of treatment as may be specified in the order, that is to say –

(a) treatment as a non-resident patient at such institution or place as may be specified in the order; and
(b) treatment by or under the direction of such registered medical practitioner as may be so specified;

but the nature of the treatment shall not be specified in the order except as mentioned in paragraph (a) or (b) above.

6 (1) Where the medical practitioner by whom or under whose direction the supervised person is being treated in pursuance of a requirement under paragraph 4 or 5 above is of the opinion that part of the treatment can be better or more conveniently given in or at an institution or place which –

(a) is not specified in the order, and
(b) is one in or at which the treatment of the supervised person will be given by or under the direction of a registered medical practitioner,

he may, with the consent of the supervised person, make arrangements for him to be treated accordingly.

(2) Such arrangements may provide for the supervised person to receive part of his treatment as a resident patient in an institution or place of any description.

(3) Where any such arrangements are made for the treatment of a supervised person –

(a) the medical practitioner by whom the arrangements are made shall give notice in writing to the supervising officer, specifying the institution or place in or at which the treatment is to be carried out; and

(b) the treatment provided for by the arrangements shall be deemed to be treatment to which he is required to submit in pursuance of the supervision order.

7 While the supervised person is under treatment as a resident patient in pursuance of arrangements under paragraph 6 above, the supervising officer shall carry out the supervision to such extent only as may be necessary for the purpose of the revocation or amendment of the order.

Requirements as to residence

8 (1) Subject to sub-paragraph (2) below, a supervision order may include requirements as to the residence of the supervised person.

(2) Before making such an order containing any such requirement, the court shall consider the home surroundings of the supervised person.

PART 3

REVOCATION AND AMENDMENT OF ORDERS

Revocation of order

9 (1) Where a supervision order is in force in respect of any person and, on the application of the supervised person or the supervising officer, it appears to a magistrates' court acting for the local justice area concerned that, having regard to circumstances which have arisen since the order was made, it would be in the interests of the health or welfare of the supervised person that the order should be revoked, the court may revoke the order.

(2) The court by which a supervision order was made may of its own motion revoke the order if, having regard to circumstances which have arisen since the order was made, it considers that it would be inappropriate for the order to continue.

Amendment of order by reason of change of residence

10 (1) This paragraph applies where, at any time while a supervision order is in force in respect of any person, a magistrates' court acting for the local justice area concerned is satisfied that the supervised person proposes to change, or has changed, his residence from the area specified in the order to another local social services authority area or local justice area.

(2) Subject to sub-paragraph (3) below, the court may, and on the application of the supervising officer shall, amend the supervision order by substituting the other area for the area specified in the order.

(3) The court shall not amend under this paragraph a supervision order which contains requirements which, in the opinion of the court, cannot be complied with unless the supervised person continues to reside in the area specified in the order unless, in accordance with paragraph 11 below, it either –

(a) cancels those requirements; or
(b) substitutes for those requirements other requirements which can be complied with if the supervised person ceases to reside in that area.

Amendment of requirements of order

11 (1) Without prejudice to the provisions of paragraph 10 above, but subject to sub-paragraph (2) below, a magistrates' court for the local justice area concerned may, on the application of the supervised person or the supervising officer, by order amend a supervision order –

(a) by cancelling any of the requirements of the order; or
(b) by inserting in the order (either in addition to or in substitution for any such requirement) any requirement which the court could include if it were the court by which the order was made and were then making it.

(2) The power of a magistrates' court under sub-paragraph (1) above shall not include power to amend an order by extending the period specified in it beyond the end of two years from the day of the original order.

Amendment of requirements in pursuance of medical report

12 (1) Where the medical practitioner by whom or under whose direction the supervised person is being treated for his mental condition in pursuance of any requirement of a supervision order –

(a) is of the opinion mentioned in sub-paragraph (2) below, or
(b) is for any reason unwilling to continue to treat or direct the treatment of the supervised person,

he shall make a report in writing to that effect to the supervising officer and that officer shall apply under paragraph 11 above to a magistrates' court for the local justice area concerned for the variation or cancellation of the requirement.

(2) The opinion referred to in sub-paragraph (1) above is –

(a) that the treatment of the supervised person should be continued beyond the period specified in the supervision order;
(b) that the supervised person needs different treatment, being treatment of a kind to which he could be required to submit in pursuance of such an order;
(c) that the supervised person is not susceptible to treatment; or
(d) that the supervised person does not require further treatment.

Supplemental

13 (1) On the making under paragraph 9 above of an order revoking a supervision order, the designated officer for the local justice area concerned, or (as the case may be) the Crown Court, shall forthwith give copies of the revoking order to the supervising officer.

(2) A supervising officer to whom in accordance with sub-paragraph (1) above copies of a revoking order are given shall give a copy to the supervised person and to the person in charge of any institution in which the supervised person is residing.

14 (1) On the making under paragraph 10 or 11 above of any order amending a supervision order, the designated officer for the local justice area concerned shall forthwith –

(a) if the order amends the supervision order otherwise than by substituting a new area or a new place for the one specified in the supervision order, give copies of the amending order to the supervising officer;

(b) if the order amends the supervision order in the manner excepted by paragraph (a) above, send to the designated officer for the new local justice area concerned –

(i) copies of the amending order; and

(ii) such documents and information relating to the case as he considers likely to be of assistance to a court acting for that area in exercising its functions in relation to the order;

and in a case falling within paragraph (b) above, the designated officer for that area shall give copies of the amending order to the supervising officer.

(2) Where the designated officer for the court making the order is also the designated officer for the new local justice area –

(a) sub-paragraph (1)(b) above does not apply; but

(b) the designated officers shall give copies of the amending order to the supervising officer.

(3) Where in accordance with sub-paragraph (1) or (2) above copies of an order are given to the supervising officer, he shall give a copy to the supervised person and to the person in charge of any institution in which the supervised person is or was residing.'

SCHEDULE 3 UNFITNESS TO STAND TRIAL AND INSANITY: COURTS-MARTIAL ETC

Section 26

Army Act 1955 (3 & 4 Eliz. 2 c. 18) and Air Force Act 1955 (3 & 4 Eliz. 2 c. 19)

1 For section 116 of the Army Act 1955 and of the Air Force Act 1955 (provisions where accused found insane) substitute –

'Findings of unfitness to stand trial and insanity

115A Fitness to stand trial

(1) This section applies where on a trial by court-martial of a person the question arises (at the instance of the defence or otherwise) whether the accused is fit to stand trial.

(2) For the purposes of this Act a person is unfit to stand trial if he is under a disability such that apart from the Criminal Procedure (Insanity) Act 1964 it would constitute a bar to his being tried on indictment in England and Wales.

(3) If, having regard to the nature of the supposed disability, the judge advocate is of opinion that it is expedient to do so and in the interests of the accused, he may

postpone consideration of the question of fitness to stand trial until any time up to the opening of the case for the defence.

(4) If, before the question of fitness to stand trial falls to be determined, the court finds the accused not guilty on the charge or each of the charges on which he is being tried, that question shall not be determined.

(5) Subject to subsections (3) and (4) above, the question of fitness to stand trial shall be determined as soon as it arises.

(6) The question of fitness to stand trial shall be determined by the judge advocate sitting alone.

(7) A judge advocate shall not make a determination under subsection (6) above except on the written or oral evidence of two or more registered medical practitioners at least one of whom is duly approved.

115B Finding that the accused did the act or made the omission charged

(1) This section applies where in accordance with section 115A(6) above it is determined by a judge advocate that the accused is unfit to stand trial.

(2) The trial shall not proceed or further proceed but it shall be determined by the court –

   (a) on the evidence (if any) already given in the trial, and
   (b) on such evidence as may be adduced or further adduced by the prosecution, or adduced by a person appointed by the judge advocate under this section to put the case for the defence,

   whether it is satisfied, as respects the charge or each of the charges on which the accused was to be or was being tried, that he did the act or made the omission charged against him as the offence.

(3) If as respects that charge or any of those charges the court is satisfied as mentioned in subsection (2) above, it shall make a finding that the accused did the act or made the omission charged against him.

(4) If as respects that charge or any of those charges the court is not so satisfied, the court shall find the accused not guilty as if on the charge in question the trial had proceeded to a conclusion.

(5) Where the question of fitness to stand trial was determined after arraignment of the accused, the determination under subsection (2) above shall be made by the court-martial by whom he was being tried.

116 Findings of insanity

(1) Where, on the trial of a person by court-martial, the court is satisfied, as respects the charge or any of the charges on which he is being tried, that the accused did the act or made the omission charged against him as the offence but that at the time of that act or omission he was insane, the court shall find that the accused was not guilty of that offence by reason of insanity.

(2) No finding under subsection (1) above shall be made except on the written or oral evidence of two or more registered medical practitioners at least one of whom is duly approved.

116A Powers to deal with person unfit to stand trial or not guilty by reason of insanity

(1) This section applies where, on a trial of a person by a court-martial –

   (a) the accused is found to be unfit to stand trial and to have done the act or made the omission charged against him; or
   (b) the accused is found not guilty by reason of insanity.

(2) The court shall make in respect of the accused –

   (a) a hospital order (with or without a restriction order);

(b) a supervision order; or
(c) an order for his absolute discharge.

(3) Where –

(a) the offence to which the finding relates is an offence the sentence for which is fixed by law, and
(b) the court has power to make a hospital order,

the court shall make a hospital order with a restriction order (whether or not it would have power to make a restriction order apart from this subsection).

(4) The functions of the court under this section shall be exercised by the judge advocate (or, where subsection (5) below applies, the judicial officer) sitting alone, and section 95(2) and (3) above shall not apply.

(5) Any function of the court under this section exercisable after an adjournment or an appeal shall be exercisable by a judicial officer if –

(a) the court ordering the adjournment, or (as the case may be) the Courts-Martial Appeal Court, so orders; or
(b) the Judge Advocate General so directs.

(6) In this Act –

"hospital order" has the meaning given in section 37 of the Mental Health Act 1983;
"restriction order" has the meaning given to it by section 41 of that Act;
"supervision order" means an order which requires the person in respect of whom it is made ("the supervised person") to be under the supervision of a person ("the supervising officer") for a period specified in the order of not more than two years.

116B Orders under the Mental Health Act

(1) In relation to the making of an order by virtue of subsection (2)(a) of section 116A above, section 37 (hospital orders etc) of the Mental Health Act 1983 ("the 1983 Act") shall have effect as if –

(a) the reference in subsection (1) to a person being convicted before the Crown Court included a reference to the case where section 116A above applies;
(b) the words after "punishable with imprisonment" and before "or is convicted" were omitted; and
(c) for subsections (4) and (5) there were substituted –

"(4) Where an order is made under this section requiring a person to be admitted to a hospital ('a hospital order'), it shall be the duty of the managers of the hospital specified in the order to admit him in accordance with it."

(2) In relation to a case where section 116A above applies but the court has not yet made one of the disposals mentioned in subsection (2) of that section –

(a) section 35 of the 1983 Act (remand to hospital for report on accused's mental condition) shall have effect with the omission of the words after paragraph (b) in subsection (3);
(b) section 36 of that Act (remand of accused person to hospital for treatment) shall have effect with the omission of the words "(other than an offence the sentence for which is fixed by law)" in subsection (2);
(c) references in sections 35 and 36 of that Act to an accused person shall be construed as including a person in whose case this subsection applies; and
(d) section 38 of that Act (interim hospital orders) shall have effect as if –

(i) the reference in subsection (1) to a person being convicted before the Crown Court included a reference to the case where section 116A above applies; and

(ii) the words "(other than an offence the sentence for which is fixed by law)" in that subsection were omitted.

(3) In relation to the making of any order under the 1983 Act by virtue of this Act, that Act shall apply –

(a) as if references to the Crown Court were references to a court-martial;
(b) as if references to an offender were references to a person in whose case section 116A above applies (references to an offence being construed accordingly); and
(c) with such further modifications as may be prescribed.

(4) The Secretary of State may by regulations make provision with respect to the admission to, detention in, and release from, hospital of any person in respect of whom an order is made under the 1983 Act by virtue of this Act.

Regulations under this subsection may in particular make provision for a person in respect of whom such an order has been made to be conveyed to, and detained in, a place of safety pending his admission to hospital.

(5) Where –

(a) a person is detained in pursuance of a hospital order which the court had power to make by virtue of section 116A(1)(a) above, and
(b) the court also made a restriction order, and that order has not ceased to have effect,

the Secretary of State, if satisfied after consultation with the responsible medical officer that the person can properly be tried, may either remit the person for trial before a court-martial or direct that he be tried before a civil court.

In this subsection "responsible medical officer" means the registered medical practitioner in charge of the person's treatment.

(6) The Secretary of State may by regulations make provision supplementing subsection (5) above, including in particular –

(a) provision for a person in whose case that subsection applies to be conveyed to a court or place of detention and to be detained in such a place;
(b) provision for the hospital order and the restriction order to cease to have effect at such time as may be prescribed.

116C Supervision orders

(1) The court shall not make an order under section 116A(2)(b) above unless it is satisfied –

(a) that, having regard to all the circumstances of the case, the making of a supervision order is the most suitable means of dealing with the accused;
(b) that the supervising officer intended to be specified in the order is willing to undertake the supervision; and
(c) that arrangements have been made for any treatment which (under subsection (2) below) is intended to be specified in the order.

(2) An order under section 116A(2)(b) above may, in accordance with regulations under subsection (3) below, require the supervised person to submit, during the whole of that period or such part of it as may be specified in the order, to treatment by or under the direction of a registered medical practitioner.

(3) The Secretary of State may –

(a) by order direct that the definition of "supervision order" in section 116A(6) above shall be amended by substituting, for the period for the time being specified there, such period as may be specified in the order under this subsection;

(b) by regulations make further provision in relation to supervision orders.

(4) Regulations under subsection (3) above may in particular make provision –

(a) as to the procedure to be followed by a court-martial making a supervision order;

(b) as the requirements which may be specified in such an order;

(c) as to the descriptions of supervising officer who may be so specified;

(d) for treatment to be provided at a place other than the place specified in the order in accordance with arrangements made by the medical practitioner by whom or under whose direction the supervised person is being treated;

(e) for the amendment and revocation of any supervision order.

116D Provisions supplementary to sections 115A to 116C

(1) In this section and sections 115A to 116C above –

"duly approved" means approved for the purposes of section 12 of the Mental Health Act 1983 by the Secretary of State as having special experience in the diagnosis and treatment of mental disorder (within the meaning of that Act);

"prescribed" means prescribed by regulations made by the Secretary of State.

(2) For the purposes of the provisions of sections 115A and 116 of this Act which permit a court to act on the written evidence of a registered medical practitioner or a registered medical practitioner who is duly approved, a report in writing purporting to be signed by a registered medical practitioner or a registered medical practitioner who is duly approved may, subject to subsection (3) below, be received in evidence without proof of the signature of the practitioner and without proof that he has the requisite qualifications or is duly approved; but the court may require the signatory of any such report to be called to give oral evidence.

(3) Where, in pursuance of a direction of the court, any such report is tendered in evidence otherwise than by or on behalf of the accused, then –

(a) if the accused is represented by counsel or a solicitor, a copy of the report shall be given to his counsel or solicitor;

(b) if the accused is not so represented, the substance of the report shall be disclosed to him; and

(c) the accused may require the signatory of the report to be called to give oral evidence, and evidence to rebut the evidence contained in the report may be called by the accused or on his behalf.

(4) The power of the Secretary of State to make regulations under sections 116A to 116C above, and orders under section 116C(3) above, shall be exercisable by statutory instrument which shall be subject to annulment in pursuance of a resolution of either House of Parliament.'

2 In section 225(1) of the Army Act 1955 and in section 223(1) of the Air Force Act 1955 (general provisions as to interpretation) insert at the appropriate places –

'"hospital order" has the meaning assigned to it by section 116A(6) of this Act;';
'"restriction order" has the meaning assigned to it by section 116A(6) of this Act;';
'"supervision order" has the meaning assigned to it by section 116A(6) of this Act;'.

Naval Discipline Act 1957 (c. 53)

3 For section 63 of the Naval Discipline Act 1957 (provisions where accused found insane) substitute –

'Findings of unfitness to stand trial and insanity

62A Fitness to stand trial

(1) This section applies where on a trial by court-martial of a person the question arises (at the instance of the defence or otherwise) whether the accused is fit to stand trial.
(2) For the purposes of this Act a person is unfit to stand trial if he is under a disability such that apart from the Criminal Procedure (Insanity) Act 1964 it would constitute a bar to his being tried on indictment in England and Wales.
(3) If, having regard to the nature of the supposed disability, the judge advocate is of opinion that it is expedient to do so and in the interests of the accused, he may postpone consideration of the question of fitness to stand trial until any time up to the opening of the case for the defence.
(4) If, before the question of fitness to stand trial falls to be determined, the court finds the accused not guilty on the charge or each of the charges on which he is being tried, that question shall not be determined.
(5) Subject to subsections (3) and (4) above, the question of fitness to stand trial shall be determined as soon as it arises.
(6) The question of fitness to stand trial shall be determined by the judge advocate sitting alone.
(7) A judge advocate shall not make a determination under subsection (6) above except on the written or oral evidence of two or more registered medical practitioners at least one of whom is duly approved.

62B Finding that the accused did the act or made the omission charged

(1) This section applies where in accordance with section 62A(6) above it is determined by a judge advocate that the accused is unfit to stand trial.
(2) The trial shall not proceed or further proceed but it shall be determined by the court –

  (a) on the evidence (if any) already given in the trial, and
  (b) on such evidence as may be adduced or further adduced by the prosecution, or adduced by a person appointed by the judge advocate under this section to put the case for the defence,

whether it is satisfied, as respects the charge or each of the charges on which the accused was to be or was being tried, that he did the act or made the omission charged against him as the offence.
(3) If as respects that charge or any of those charges the court is satisfied as mentioned in subsection (2) above, it shall make a finding that the accused did the act or made the omission charged against him.
(4) If as respects that charge or any of those charges the court is not so satisfied, the court shall find the accused not guilty as if on the charge in question the trial had proceeded to a conclusion.
(5) Where the question of fitness to stand trial was determined after arraignment of the accused, the determination under subsection (2) above shall be made by the court-martial by whom he was being tried.

63 Findings of insanity

(1) Where, on the trial of a person by court-martial, the court is satisfied, as respects the charge or any of the charges on which he is being tried, that the accused did the act or made the omission charged against him as the offence but that at the time of that act or omission he was insane, the court shall find that the accused was not guilty of that offence by reason of insanity.

(2) No finding under subsection (1) above shall be made except on the written or oral evidence of two or more registered medical practitioners at least one of whom is duly approved.

63A Powers to deal with person unfit to stand trial or not guilty by reason of insanity

(1) This section applies where, on a trial of a person by a court-martial –

(a) the accused is found to be unfit to stand trial and to have done the act or made the omission charged against him; or

(b) the accused is found not guilty by reason of insanity.

(2) The court shall make in respect of the accused –

(a) a hospital order (with or without a restriction order);

(b) a supervision order; or

(c) an order for his absolute discharge.

(3) Where –

(a) the offence to which the finding relates is an offence the sentence for which is fixed by law, and

(b) the court has power to make a hospital order,

the court shall make a hospital order with a restriction order (whether or not it would have power to make a restriction order apart from this subsection).

(4) The functions of the court under this section shall be exercised by the judge advocate (or, where subsection (5) below applies, the judicial officer) sitting alone, and sections 56A(3) and 57 above shall not apply.

(5) Any function of the court under this section exercisable after an adjournment or an appeal shall be exercisable by a judicial officer if –

(a) the court ordering the adjournment, or (as the case may be) the Courts-Martial Appeal Court, so orders; or

(b) the Judge Advocate of Her Majesty's Fleet so directs.

(6) In this Act –

"hospital order" has the meaning given in section 37 of the Mental Health Act 1983;

"restriction order" has the meaning given to it by section 41 of that Act;

"supervision order" means an order which requires the person in respect of whom it is made ("the supervised person") to be under the supervision of a person ("the supervising officer") for a period specified in the order of not more than two years.

63B Orders under the Mental Health Act

(1) In relation to the making of an order by virtue of subsection (2)(a) of section 63A above, section 37 (hospital orders etc) of the Mental Health Act 1983 ("the 1983 Act") shall have effect as if –

(a) the reference in subsection (1) to a person being convicted before the Crown Court included a reference to the case where section 63A above applies;

(b) the words after "punishable with imprisonment" and before "or is convicted" were omitted; and

(c) for subsections (4) and (5) there were substituted –

"(4) Where an order is made under this section requiring a person to be admitted to a hospital ('a hospital order'), it shall be the duty of the managers of the hospital specified in the order to admit him in accordance with it."

(2) In relation to a case where section 63A above applies but the court has not yet made one of the disposals mentioned in subsection (2) of that section –

(a) section 35 of the 1983 Act (remand to hospital for report on accused's mental condition) shall have effect with the omission of the words after paragraph (b) in subsection (3);
(b) section 36 of that Act (remand of accused person to hospital for treatment) shall have effect with the omission of the words "(other than an offence the sentence for which is fixed by law)" in subsection (2);
(c) references in sections 35 and 36 of that Act to an accused person shall be construed as including a person in whose case this subsection applies; and
(d) section 38 of that Act (interim hospital orders) shall have effect as if –

(i) the reference in subsection (1) to a person being convicted before the Crown Court included a reference to the case where section 63A above applies; and
(ii) the words "(other than an offence the sentence for which is fixed by law)" in that subsection were omitted.

(3) In relation to the making of any order under the 1983 Act by virtue of this Act, that Act shall apply –

(a) as if references to the Crown Court were references to a court-martial;
(b) as if references to an offender were references to a person in whose case section 63A above applies (references to an offence being construed accordingly); and
(c) with such further modifications as may be prescribed.

(4) The Secretary of State may by regulations make provision with respect to the admission to, detention in, and release from, hospital of any person in respect of whom an order is made under the 1983 Act by virtue of this Act.

Regulations under this subsection may in particular make provision for a person in respect of whom such an order has been made to be conveyed to, and detained in, a place of safety pending his admission to hospital.

(5) Where –

(a) a person is detained in pursuance of a hospital order which the court had power to make by virtue of section 63A(1)(a) above, and
(b) the court also made a restriction order, and that order has not ceased to have effect,

the Secretary of State, if satisfied after consultation with the responsible medical officer that the person can properly be tried, may either remit the person for trial before a court-martial or direct that he be tried before a civil court.

In this subsection "responsible medical officer" means the registered medical practitioner in charge of the person's treatment.

(6) The Secretary of State may by regulations make provision supplementing subsection (5) above, including in particular –

(a) provision for a person in whose case that subsection applies to be conveyed to a court or place of detention and to be detained in such a place;
(b) provision for the hospital order and the restriction order to cease to have effect at such time as may be prescribed.

63C Supervision orders

(1) The court shall not make an order under section 63A(2)(b) above unless it is satisfied –

- (a) that, having regard to all the circumstances of the case, the making of a supervision order is the most suitable means of dealing with the accused;
- (b) that the supervising officer intended to be specified in the order is willing to undertake the supervision; and
- (c) that arrangements have been made for any treatment which (under subsection (2) below) is intended to be specified in the order.

(2) An order under section 63A(2)(b) above may, in accordance with regulations under subsection (3) below, require the supervised person to submit, during the whole of that period or such part of it as may be specified in the order, to treatment by or under the direction of a registered medical practitioner.

(3) The Secretary of State may –

- (a) by order direct that the definition of "supervision order" in section 63A(6) above shall be amended by substituting, for the period for the time being specified there, such period as may be specified in the order under this subsection;
- (b) by regulations make further provision in relation to supervision orders.

(4) Regulations under subsection (3) above may in particular make provision –

- (a) as to the procedure to be followed by a court-martial making a supervision order;
- (b) as the requirements which may be specified in such an order;
- (c) as to the descriptions of supervising officer who may be so specified;
- (d) for treatment to be provided at a place other than the place specified in the order in accordance with arrangements made by the medical practitioner by whom or under whose direction the supervised person is being treated;
- (e) for the amendment and revocation of any supervision order.

63D Provisions supplementary to sections 62A to 63C

(1) In this section and sections 62A to 63C above –

"duly approved" means approved for the purposes of section 12 of the Mental Health Act 1983 by the Secretary of State as having special experience in the diagnosis and treatment of mental disorder (within the meaning of that Act);

"prescribed" means prescribed by regulations made by the Secretary of State.

(2) For the purposes of the provisions of sections 62A and 63 of this Act which permit a court to act on the written evidence of a registered medical practitioner or a registered medical practitioner who is duly approved, a report in writing purporting to be signed by a registered medical practitioner or a registered medical practitioner who is duly approved may, subject to subsection (3) below, be received in evidence without proof of the signature of the practitioner and without proof that he has the requisite qualifications or is duly approved; but the court may require the signatory of any such report to be called to give oral evidence.

(3) Where, in pursuance of a direction of the court, any such report is tendered in evidence otherwise than by or on behalf of the accused, then –

- (a) if the accused is represented by counsel or a solicitor, a copy of the report shall be given to his counsel or solicitor;
- (b) if the accused is not so represented, the substance of the report shall be disclosed to him; and

(c) the accused may require the signatory of the report to be called to give oral evidence, and evidence to rebut the evidence contained in the report may be called by the accused or on his behalf.

(4) The power of the Secretary of State to make regulations under sections 63A to 63C above, and orders under section 63C(3) above, shall be exercisable by statutory instrument which shall be subject to annulment in pursuance of a resolution of either House of Parliament.'

4 In the proviso to section 56(3) of that Act (court-martial not to be adjourned for more than six days), after 'except with the consent of the accused and the prosecuting authority' insert ', or for the purpose of exercising powers under section 63A of this Act,'.

5 In section 135(1) of that Act (general provisions as to interpretation) insert at the appropriate places –

'"hospital order" has the meaning assigned to it by section 63A(6) of this Act;';
'"restriction order" has the meaning assigned to it by section 63A(6) of this Act;';
'"supervision order" has the meaning assigned to it by section 63A(6) of this Act;'.

Courts-Martial (Appeals) Act 1968 (c. 20)

6 The Courts-Martial (Appeals) Act 1968 is amended as follows.
7 For section 16 substitute –

'16 Substitution of finding of insanity or findings of unfitness to stand trial etc.

(1) This section applies where, on an appeal against conviction, the Appeal Court, on the written or oral evidence of two or more registered medical practitioners at least one of whom is duly approved, are of opinion –

(a) that the proper finding would have been one of not guilty by reason of insanity; or
(b) that the case is not one where there should have been a finding of not guilty, but that there should have been findings that the accused was unfit to stand trial and that he did the act or made the omission charged against him.

(2) The Appeal Court shall make in respect of the appellant –

(a) a hospital order (with or without a restriction order);
(b) a supervision order; or
(c) an order for his absolute discharge.

(3) Where –

(a) the offence to which the appeal relates is an offence the sentence for which is fixed by law, and
(b) the Appeal Court have power to make a hospital order,

the Appeal Court shall make a hospital order with a restriction order (whether or not they would have power to make a restriction order apart from this subsection).

(4) The provisions of, or made under, the sections specified below shall apply (with any necessary modifications) in relation to the Appeal Court as they apply in relation to a court-martial.
The sections are –

(c) where the relevant Service Act is the Army Act, sections 116B to 116D of that Act;
(d) where the relevant Service Act is the Air Force Act, sections 116B to 116D of that Act;

(e) where the relevant Service Act is the Naval Discipline Act, sections 63B to 63D of that Act.

(5) Where the Appeal Court make an interim hospital order by virtue of this section –

(a) the power of renewing or terminating it and of dealing with the appellant on its termination shall be exercisable by a judicial officer and not by the Appeal Court; and

(b) section 38(7) of the Mental Health Act 1983 (absconding offenders) shall have effect as if the reference to the court that made the order were a reference to a judicial officer.

(6) Where the Appeal Court make a supervision order by virtue of this section, any power of revoking or amending it shall be exercisable by a judicial officer and not by the Appeal Court.'

8 In section 21 (appeal against finding of not guilty by reason of insanity), in subsection (1), after 'except' insert 'section 8(2) and'.

9 In section 22 (consequences where appeal under section 21 allowed), at the beginning of subsection (4) insert 'Subject to section 23 below,'.

10 For section 23 substitute –

'23 Substitution of findings of unfitness to stand trial etc.

(1) This section applies where, on an appeal under section 21 of this Act, the Appeal Court, on the written or oral evidence of two or more registered medical practitioners at least one of whom is duly approved, are of opinion that –

(a) the case is not one where there should have been a finding of not guilty; but

(b) there should have been findings that the accused was unfit to stand trial and that he did the act or made the omission charged against him.

(2) The Appeal Court shall make in respect of the appellant –

(a) a hospital order (with or without a restriction order);

(b) a supervision order; or

(c) an order for his absolute discharge.

(3) Where –

(a) the offence to which the appeal relates is an offence the sentence for which is fixed by law, and

(b) the Appeal Court have power to make a hospital order,

the Appeal Court shall make a hospital order with a restriction order (whether or not they would have power to make a restriction order apart from this subsection).

(4) The provisions of, or made under, the sections specified below shall apply (with any necessary modifications) in relation to the Appeal Court as they apply in relation to a court-martial.
The sections are –

(c) where the relevant Service Act is the Army Act, sections 116B to 116D of that Act;

(d) where the relevant Service Act is the Air Force Act, sections 116B to 116D of that Act;

(e) where the relevant Service Act is the Naval Discipline Act, sections 63B to 63D of that Act.

(5) Where the Appeal Court make an interim hospital order by virtue of this section –

(a) the power of renewing or terminating it and of dealing with the appellant on its termination shall be exercisable by a judicial officer and not by the Appeal Court; and
(b) section 38(7) of the Mental Health Act 1983 (absconding offenders) shall have effect as if the reference to the court that made the order were a reference to a judicial officer.

(6) Where the Appeal Court make a supervision order by virtue of this section, any power of revoking or amending it shall be exercisable by a judicial officer and not by the Appeal Court.'

11 (1) Section 24 (appeal against finding of unfitness to stand trial) is amended as follows.
(2) In subsection (1) –

(a) for 'his trial' substitute 'trial and to have done the act or made the omission charged against him';
(b) for 'the finding' substitute 'either or both of those findings'.

(3) In subsection (2), after 'except' insert 'section 8(2) and'.

12 For section 25 substitute –

'25 Disposal of appeal under s.24

(1) This section applies to appeals under section 24 of this Act.
(2) Where the Appeal Court allow an appeal against a finding that the appellant is unfit to stand trial –

(a) the appellant may be tried accordingly for the offence with which he was charged; and
(b) the Court may make such orders as appear to them necessary or expedient pending any such trial for the custody, release or continued detention of the appellant.

(3) Where, otherwise than in a case falling within subsection (2) above, the Appeal Court allow an appeal against a finding that the appellant did the act or made the omission charged against him, the Court shall, in addition to quashing the finding, direct a finding of not guilty to be recorded (but not a finding of not guilty by reason of insanity).'

13 After that section insert –

'Appeal against order made in cases of insanity or unfitness to stand trial

25A Right of appeal against hospital order etc.

(1) A person in whose case a court-martial –

(a) makes a hospital order or interim hospital order by virtue of the relevant Service Act, or
(b) makes a supervision order under the relevant Service Act,

may appeal to the Appeal Court against the order.

(2) An appeal under this section lies only with the leave of the Appeal Court.

25B Disposal of appeal under s.25A

(1) If on an appeal under section 25A of this Act the Appeal Court consider that the appellant should be dealt with differently from the way in which the court below dealt with him –

(a) they may quash any order which is the subject of the appeal; and
(b) they may make such order, whether by substitution for the original order or by variation of or addition to it, as they think appropriate for the case and as the court below had power to make.

(2) The fact that an appeal is pending against an interim hospital order under the Mental Health Act 1983 shall not affect the power of the court below to renew or terminate the order or deal with the appellant on its termination.

(3) Where the Appeal Court make an interim hospital order by virtue of this section –

(a) the power of renewing or terminating it and of dealing with the appellant on its termination shall be exercisable by a judicial officer and not by the Appeal Court; and

(b) section 38(7) of the said Act of 1983 (absconding offenders) shall have effect as if the reference to the court that made the order were a reference to a judicial officer.

(4) The fact that an appeal is pending against a supervision order under the relevant Service Act shall not affect any power conferred on any other court to revoke or amend the order.

(5) Where the Appeal Court make a supervision order by virtue of this section, any power of revoking or amending it shall be exercisable by a judicial officer and not by the Appeal Court.'

14 (1) Section 57 (interpretation) is amended as follows.

(2) In subsection (1) insert at the relevant places –

'"duly approved" means approved for the purposes of section 12 of the Mental Health Act 1983 by the Secretary of State as having special experience in the diagnosis and treatment of mental disorder (within the meaning of that Act);';

'"hospital order" has the meaning given in section 37 of the Mental Health Act 1983;';

'"interim hospital order" has the meaning given in section 38 of that Act;';

'"judicial officer" has the same meaning as in the relevant Service Act;';

'"restriction order" has the meaning given to it by section 41 of the Mental Health Act 1983;';

'"supervision order" means an order which requires the person in respect of whom it is made to be under the supervision of another person for a period specified in the order of not more than two years.'

(3) After subsection (2) insert –

'(2A) For the purposes of the provisions of sections 16 and 23 of this Act which permit the Appeal Court to act on the written evidence of a registered medical practitioner or a registered medical practitioner who is duly approved, a report in writing purporting to be signed by a registered medical practitioner or a registered medical practitioner who is duly approved may, subject to subsection (2B) below, be received in evidence without proof of the signature of the practitioner and without proof that he has the requisite qualifications or is duly approved; but the Appeal Court may require the signatory of any such report to be called to give oral evidence.

(2B) Where, in pursuance of a direction of the Appeal Court, any such report is tendered in evidence otherwise than by or on behalf of the appellant, then –

(a) if the appellant is represented by counsel or a solicitor, a copy of the report shall be given to his counsel or solicitor;

(b) if the appellant is not so represented, the substance of the report shall be disclosed to him; and

(c) the appellant may require the signatory of the report to be called to give oral evidence, and evidence to rebut the evidence contained in the report may be called by the appellant or on his behalf.'

15 (1) Schedule 3 (modifications in relation to prisoners of war) is amended as follows.

(2) In paragraph 3 –

(a) in paragraph (a), for 'or 15' substitute ', 14A, 15 or 25A';

(b) omit paragraph (b).

(3) After paragraph 3 insert –

'3A In relation to a protected prisoner of war, sections 16 and 23 of this Act shall each have effect as if the following subsection were substituted for subsection (4) –

"(4) The provisions of a Royal Warrant shall apply (with any necessary modifications) in relation to the Appeal Court as they apply in relation to a court-martial."'

SCHEDULE 4 POWERS OF AUTHORISED OFFICERS EXECUTING WARRANTS

Section 27

The following is the Schedule inserted after Schedule 4 to the Magistrates' Courts Act 1980 (c. 43) –

'SCHEDULE 4A POWERS OF AUTHORISED OFFICERS EXECUTING WARRANTS

Section 125BA

Meaning of 'authorised officer' etc

1 In this Schedule –

"authorised officer", in relation to a warrant, means a person who is entitled to execute the warrant by virtue of –

(a) section 125A of this Act (civilian enforcement officers); or

(b) section 125B of this Act (approved enforcement agencies);

"premises" includes any place and, in particular, includes –

(a) any vehicle, vessel, aircraft or hovercraft;

(b) any offshore installation within the meaning of the Mineral Workings (Offshore Installations) Act 1971; and

(c) any tent or movable structure.

Entry to execute warrant of arrest etc

2 (1) An authorised officer may enter and search any premises for the purpose of executing a warrant of arrest, commitment or detention issued in proceedings for or in connection with any criminal offence.

(2) The power may be exercised –

(a) only to the extent that it is reasonably required for that purpose; and

(b) only if the officer has reasonable grounds for believing that the person whom he is seeking is on the premises.

(3) In relation to premises consisting of two or more separate dwellings, the power is limited to entering and searching –

(a) any parts of the premises which the occupiers of any dwelling comprised in the premises use in common with the occupiers of any other such dwelling; and

(b) any such dwelling in which the officer has reasonable grounds for believing that the person whom he is seeking may be.

Entry to levy distress

3 (1) An authorised officer may enter and search any premises for the purpose of executing a warrant of distress issued under section 76 of this Act for default in paying a sum adjudged to be paid by a conviction.

(2) The power may be exercised only to the extent that it is reasonably required for that purpose.

Searching arrested persons

4 (1) This paragraph applies where a person is arrested in pursuance of a warrant of arrest, commitment or detention issued in proceedings for or in connection with any criminal offence.

(2) An authorised officer may search the arrested person, if he has reasonable grounds for believing that the arrested person may present a danger to himself or others.

(3) An authorised officer may also search the arrested person for anything which he might use to assist him to escape from lawful custody.

(4) The power conferred by sub-paragraph (3) above may be exercised –

(a) only if the officer has reasonable grounds for believing that the arrested person may have concealed on him anything of a kind mentioned in that sub-paragraph; and

(b) only to the extent that it is reasonably required for the purpose of discovering any such thing.

(5) The powers conferred by this paragraph to search a person are not to be read as authorising the officer to require a person to remove any of his clothing in public other than an outer coat, a jacket or gloves; but they do authorise the search of a person's mouth.

(6) An officer searching a person under sub-paragraph (2) above may seize and retain anything he finds, if the officer has reasonable grounds for believing that the person searched might use it to cause physical injury to himself or to any other person.

(7) An officer searching a person under sub-paragraph (3) above may seize and retain anything he finds, if he has reasonable grounds for believing that the person might use it to assist him to escape from lawful custody.

Use of force

5 An authorised officer may use reasonable force, if necessary, in the exercise of a power conferred on him by this Schedule.'

SCHEDULE 5 PROCEDURE ON BREACH OF COMMUNITY PENALTY ETC

Section 29

Interpretation

1 In this Schedule –

'the Sentencing Act' means the Powers of Criminal Courts (Sentencing) Act 2000 (c. 6);

'the 2003 Act' means the Criminal Justice Act 2003 (c. 44).

Detention and training orders

2 (1) Section 104 of the Sentencing Act (breach of supervision requirements of detention and training order) is amended as follows.

(2) In subsection (1) (issue of summons or warrant by justice of the peace) –

(a) omit the words 'acting for a relevant petty sessions area';

(b) in paragraph (a), omit the words 'before a youth court acting for the area';

(c) in paragraph (b), omit the words 'requiring him to be brought before such a court'.

(3) For subsection (2) substitute –

'(2) Any summons or warrant issued under this section shall direct the offender to appear or be brought –

(a) before a youth court acting for the petty sessions area in which the offender resides; or

(b) if it is not known where the offender resides, before a youth court acting for same petty sessions area as the justice who issued the summons or warrant.'

Suspended sentence supervision orders

3 (1) Section 123 of the Sentencing Act (breach of requirement of suspended sentence supervision order) is amended as follows.

(2) In subsection (1) (issue of summons or warrant by justice of the peace) omit the words 'acting for the petty sessions area for the time being specified in the order'.

(3) For subsection (2) substitute –

'(2) Any summons or warrant issued under this section shall direct the offender to appear or be brought –

(a) before a magistrates' court for the petty sessions area in which the offender resides; or

(b) if it is not known where the offender resides, before a magistrates' court acting for the petty sessions area for the time being specified in the suspended sentence supervision order.'

(4) After subsection (4) insert –

'(5) Where a magistrates' court dealing with an offender under this section would not otherwise have the power to amend the suspended sentence supervision order under section 124(3) below (amendment by reason of change of residence), that provision has effect as if the reference to a magistrates' court acting for the petty sessions area for the time being specified in the suspended sentence supervision order were a reference to the court dealing with the offender.'

Community orders under the Sentencing Act

4 (1) Schedule 3 to the Sentencing Act (breach, revocation and amendment of certain community orders), as it has effect on the day on which this Act is passed, is amended as follows.

(2) In paragraph 3(1) (issue of summons or warrant by justice of the peace) omit the words 'acting for the petty sessions area concerned'.

(3) In paragraph 3(2) (court before which offender to appear or be brought), for paragraph (c) substitute –

'(c) in the case of a relevant order which is not an order to which paragraph (a) or (b) applies, before a magistrates' court acting for the petty sessions area in which the offender resides or, if it is not known where he resides, before a magistrates' court acting for the petty sessions area concerned.'

(4) In paragraph 4 (powers of magistrates' court to deal with breach), after sub-paragraph (3) insert –

'(3A) Where a magistrates' court dealing with an offender under sub-paragraph (1)(a), (b) or (c) above would not otherwise have the power to amend the relevant order under paragraph 18 below (amendment by reason of change of residence), that paragraph has effect as if the reference to a magistrates' court acting for the petty sessions area concerned were a reference to the court dealing with the offender.'

Curfew orders and exclusion orders

5 (1) Schedule 3 to the Sentencing Act (breach, revocation and amendment of curfew orders and exclusion orders), as substituted by paragraph 125 of Schedule 32 to the 2003 Act, is amended as follows.

(2) In paragraph 3(1) (issue of summons or warrant by justice of the peace) omit the words 'acting for the petty sessions area concerned'.

(3) In paragraph 3(2) (court before which offender to appear or be brought), for paragraph (b) substitute –

'(b) in the case of a relevant order which is not an order to which paragraph (a) above applies, before a magistrates' court acting for the petty sessions area in which the offender resides or, if it is not known where he resides, before a magistrates' court acting for the petty sessions area concerned.'

(4) In paragraph 4 (powers of magistrates' court to deal with breach), after sub-paragraph (4) insert –

'(4A) Where a magistrates' court dealing with an offender under sub-paragraph (2)(a) or (b) above would not otherwise have the power to amend the relevant order under paragraph 15 below (amendment by reason of change of residence), that paragraph has effect as if the reference to a magistrates' court acting for the petty sessions area concerned were a reference to the court dealing with the offender.'

Attendance centre orders

6 (1) Schedule 5 to the Sentencing Act (breach, revocation and amendment of attendance centre orders) is amended as follows.

(2) In paragraph 1(1) (issue of summons or warrant by justice of the peace), omit the words –

(a) 'acting for a relevant petty sessions area';
(b) 'before a magistrates' court acting for the area';
(c) 'requiring him to be brought before such a court'.

(3) For paragraph 1(2) substitute –

'(2) Any summons or warrant issued under this paragraph shall direct the offender to appear or be brought –

(a) before a magistrates' court acting for the petty sessions area in which the offender resides; or

(b) if it is not known where the offender resides, before a magistrates' court acting for the petty sessions area in which is situated the attendance centre which the offender is required to attend by the order or by virtue of an order under paragraph 5(1)(b) below.'

(4) In paragraph 2 (powers of magistrates' court to deal with breach), after sub-paragraph (5) insert –

'(5A) Where a magistrates' court dealing with an offender under sub-paragraph (1)(a) above would not otherwise have the power to amend the order under paragraph 5(1)(b) below (substitution of different attendance centre), that paragraph has effect as if references to an appropriate magistrates' court were references to the court dealing with the offender.'

Community orders under the 2003 Act

7 (1) Schedule 8 to the 2003 Act (breach, revocation or amendment of community order) is amended as follows.

(2) In paragraph 7(2) (issue of summons or warrant by justice of the peace) omit the words 'acting for the petty sessions area concerned'.

(3) In paragraph 7(3) (court before which offender to appear or be brought), for paragraph (b) substitute –

'(b) in any other case, before a magistrates' court acting for the petty sessions area in which the offender resides or, if it is not known where he resides, before a magistrates' court acting for the petty sessions area concerned.'

(4) In paragraph 9 (powers of magistrates' court to deal with breach), after sub-paragraph (5) insert –

'(5A) Where a magistrates' court dealing with an offender under sub-paragraph (1)(a) would not otherwise have the power to amend the community order under paragraph 16 (amendment by reason of change of residence), that paragraph has effect as if the references to the appropriate court were references to the court dealing with the offender.'

(5) In paragraph 27 (provision of copies of orders), at the end of sub-paragraph (1)(c) insert ', and

(d) where the court acts for a petty sessions area other than the one specified in the order prior to the revocation or amendment, provide a copy of the revoking or amending order to a magistrates' court acting for the area so specified.'

Suspended sentence orders under the 2003 Act

8 (1) Schedule 12 to the 2003 Act (breach or amendment of suspended sentence order, and effect of further conviction) is amended as follows.

(2) In paragraph 6(2) (issue of summons or warrant by justice of the peace) omit the words 'acting for the petty sessions area concerned'.

(3) In paragraph 6(3) (court before which offender to appear or be brought), for paragraph (b) substitute –

'(b) in any other case, before a magistrates' court acting for the petty sessions area in which the offender resides or, if it is not known where he resides, before a magistrates' court acting for the petty sessions area concerned.'

(4) In paragraph 8 (powers of magistrates' court to deal with breach), after sub-paragraph (4) insert –

'(4A) Where a magistrates' court dealing with an offender under sub-paragraph (2)(c) would not otherwise have the power to amend the suspended sentence order under paragraph 14 (amendment by reason of change of residence), that paragraph has effect as if the references to the appropriate court were references to the court dealing with the offender.'

(5) In paragraph 22 (provision of copies of orders), at the end of sub-paragraph (1)(c) insert ', and

(d) where the court acts for a petty sessions area other than the one specified in the order prior to the revocation or amendment, provide a copy of the revoking or amending order to a magistrates' court acting for the area so specified.'

9 In Schedule 13 to the 2003 Act (transfer of suspended sentence orders to Scotland or Northern Ireland), in paragraph 12 (modifications of Schedule 12), after sub-paragraph (5) insert –

'(5A) In paragraph 6(3)(b), the words "before a magistrates" court acting for the petty sessions area in which the offender resides or, if it is not known where he resides,' are omitted.'

Local justice areas

10 The power conferred by section 109(5)(b) of the Courts Act 2003 (c. 39) to amend or repeal any enactment, other than one contained in an Act passed in a later session, includes power to amend any such enactment as amended by this Schedule, but only for the purpose of making consequential provision in connection with the establishment of local justice areas under section 8 of that Act.

SCHEDULE 6 INTERMITTENT CUSTODY

Section 31

1 The Criminal Justice Act 2003 (c. 44) is amended as follows.

2 In section 244 (duty to release prisoners), in subsection (3) –

(a) in paragraph (c), for the words from 'which is not' to 'section 183(3)' substitute 'which for the purposes of section 183 (as read with section 263(2) or 264A(2) in the case of concurrent or consecutive sentences) is not a licence period';

(b) in paragraph (d), after 'consecutive sentences' insert 'none of which falls within paragraph (c)'.

3 In section 246 (power to release prisoners on licence before required to do so), in the definition of 'the required custodial days' in subsection (6) –

(a) in paragraph (b), after 'custody' insert 'which are consecutive';

(b) at the end of that paragraph insert ', or

(c) in the case of two or more sentences of intermittent custody which are wholly or partly concurrent, the aggregate of the numbers so specified less the number of days that are to be served concurrently;'.

4 In section 249 (duration of licence), at the end of subsection (3) insert 'and subsection (2) has effect subject to section 264A(3) (consecutive terms: intermittent custody)'.

5 In section 250 (licence conditions), in subsection (7), for 'and section 264(3) and (4) (consecutive terms)' substitute ', section 264(3) and (4) (consecutive terms) and section 264A(3) (consecutive terms: intermittent custody)'.

6 In section 264 (consecutive terms), in subsection (1), after paragraph (b) insert ', and

(c) none of those terms is a term to which an intermittent custody order relates.'

7 After that section insert –

'264A Consecutive terms: intermittent custody

(1) This section applies where –

(a) a person ("the offender") has been sentenced to two or more terms of imprisonment which are to be served consecutively on each other,

(b) the sentences were passed on the same occasion or, where they were passed on different occasions, the person has not been released under this Chapter at any time during the period beginning with the first and ending with the last of those occasions, and

(c) each of the terms is a term to which an intermittent custody order relates.

(2) The offender is not to be treated as having served all the required custodial days in relation to any of the terms of imprisonment until he has served the aggregate of all the required custodial days in relation to each of them.

(3) After the number of days served by the offender in prison is equal to the aggregate of the required custodial days in relation to each of the terms of imprisonment, the offender is to be on licence until the relevant time and subject to such conditions as are required by this Chapter in respect of any of the terms of imprisonment, and none of the terms is to be regarded for any purpose as continuing after the relevant time.

(4) In subsection (3) "the relevant time" means the time when the offender would, but for his release, have served a term equal in length to the aggregate of –

(a) all the required custodial days in relation to the terms of imprisonment, and

(b) the longest of the total licence periods in relation to those terms.

(5) In this section –

"total licence period", in relation to a term of imprisonment to which an intermittent custody order relates, means a period equal in length to the aggregate of all the licence periods as defined by section 183 in relation to that term;

"the required custodial days", in relation to such a term, means the number of days specified under that section.'

SCHEDULE 7 INVESTIGATIONS BY PARLIAMENTARY COMMISSIONER

Section 47

1 The Parliamentary Commissioner Act 1967 (c. 13) is amended as follows.

2 (1) Section 5 (matters subject to investigation) is amended as follows.

(2) After subsection (1) insert –

'(1A) Subsection (1C) of this section applies if –

(a) a written complaint is duly made to a member of the House of Commons by a member of the public who claims that a person has failed to perform a relevant duty owed by him to the member of the public, and

(b) the complaint is referred to the Commissioner, with the consent of the person who made it, by a member of the House of Commons with a request to conduct an investigation into it.

(1B) For the purposes of subsection (1A) of this section a relevant duty is a duty imposed by any of these –

(a) a code of practice issued under section 32 of the Domestic Violence, Crime and Victims Act 2004 (code of practice for victims), or

(b) sections 35 to 44 of that Act (duties of local probation boards in connection with victims of sexual or violent offences).

(1C) If this subsection applies, the Commissioner may investigate the complaint.'

(3) In subsection (3) for 'investigation under this Act' substitute 'investigation under subsection (1) of this section'.

(4) After subsection (4) insert –

'(4A) Without prejudice to subsection (2) of this section, the Commissioner shall not conduct an investigation pursuant to a complaint under subsection (1A) of this section in respect of –

(a) action taken by or with the authority of the Secretary of State for the purposes of protecting the security of the State, including action so taken with respect to passports, or

(b) any action or matter described in any of paragraphs 1 to 4 and 6A to 11 of Schedule 3 to this Act.

(4B) Her Majesty may by Order in Council amend subsection (4A) of this section so as to exclude from paragraph (a) or (b) of that subsection such actions or matters as may be described in the Order.

(4C) Any statutory instrument made by virtue of subsection (4B) of this section shall be subject to annulment in pursuance of a resolution of either House of Parliament.'

3 (1) Section 7 (procedure in respect of investigations) is amended as follows.

(2) In subsection (1) after 'complaint under' insert 'section 5(1) of'.

(3) After subsection (1) insert –

'(1A) Where the Commissioner proposes to conduct an investigation pursuant to a complaint under section 5(1A) of this Act, he shall give the person to whom the complaint relates an opportunity to comment on any allegations contained in the complaint.'

(4) In subsection (2) for 'such investigation' substitute 'investigation under this Act'.

(5) In subsection (4) –

(a) after 'authority concerned' insert 'or the person to whom the complaint relates';

(b) for 'that department or authority' substitute 'that department, authority or person'.

4 (1) Section 8 (evidence) is amended as follows.

(2) In subsection (1) after 'investigation under' insert 'section 5(1) of'.

(3) After subsection (1) insert –

'(1A) For the purposes of an investigation pursuant to a complaint under section 5(1A) of this Act the Commissioner may require any person who in his opinion is able to furnish information or produce documents relevant to the investigation to furnish any such information or produce any such document.'

(4) In subsection (2) for 'such investigation' substitute 'investigation under this Act'.

5 (1) Section 10 (reports by Commissioner) is amended as follows.
(2) In subsection (2), after 'investigation under' insert 'section 5(1) of'.
(3) After subsection (2) insert –

'(2A) In any case where the Commissioner conducts an investigation pursuant to a complaint under section 5(1A) of this Act, he shall also send a report of the results of the investigation to the person to whom the complaint relates.'

(4) In subsection (3) after 'investigation under' insert 'section 5(1) of'.
(5) After subsection (3) insert –

'(3A) If, after conducting an investigation pursuant to a complaint under section 5(1A) of this Act, it appears to the Commissioner that –

(a) the person to whom the complaint relates has failed to perform a relevant duty owed by him to the person aggrieved, and
(b) the failure has not been, or will not be, remedied,

the Commissioner may, if he thinks fit, lay before each House of Parliament a special report upon the case.

(3B) For the purposes of subsection (3A) of this section 'relevant duty' has the meaning given by section 5(1B) of this Act.'

(6) In subsection (5)(d) after 'subsection (2)' insert 'or (2A)'.

6 In section 12(1) (interpretation) for the definition of 'person aggrieved' substitute –

'"person aggrieved" –
(a) in relation to a complaint under section 5(1) of this Act, means the person who claims or is alleged to have sustained such injustice as is mentioned in section 5(1)(a) of this Act;
(b) in relation to a complaint under section 5(1A) of this Act, means the person to whom the duty referred to in section 5(1A)(a) of this Act is or is alleged to be owed;'.

SCHEDULE 8 COMMISSIONER FOR VICTIMS AND WITNESSES

Section 48

Deputy Commissioner

1 (1) The Secretary of State must appoint a Deputy Commissioner for Victims and Witnesses (referred to in this Schedule as the Deputy Commissioner).
(2) Before appointing the Deputy Commissioner the Secretary of State must consult the Attorney General and the Lord Chancellor as to the person to be appointed.
(3) The Deputy Commissioner must act as the Commissioner –

(a) during any period when the office of Commissioner is vacant;
(b) at any time when the Commissioner is absent or is unable to act.

(4) The Deputy Commissioner is not to be regarded –

(a) as the servant or agent of the Crown, or
(b) as enjoying any status, immunity or privilege of the Crown.

Terms of appointment

2 (1) This paragraph applies in relation to a person appointed as the Commissioner or the Deputy Commissioner.
(2) The period for which the person is appointed must not exceed 5 years.

(3) Subject to sub-paragraph (4), the person is eligible for re-appointment.
(4) The person must not hold office for more than 10 years in total.
(5) The person may at any time resign from office by giving notice in writing to the Secretary of State.
(6) The Secretary of State may at any time remove the person from office if he is satisfied that the person –
(a) has become bankrupt, has had his estate sequestrated or has made a composition or arrangement with, or granted a trust deed for, his creditors, or
(b) is otherwise unable or unfit to carry out his functions.
(7) The Secretary of State must consult the Attorney General and the Lord Chancellor before removing the person from office.
(8) Subject to sub-paragraphs (2) to (7), the person holds office on the terms specified by the Secretary of State after consulting the Attorney General and the Lord Chancellor.

Staff

3 (1) The Commissioner may appoint such persons as members of his staff as he thinks fit.
(2) The Commissioner must obtain the approval of the Secretary of State to –
(a) the number of persons appointed as members of his staff, and
(b) their terms and conditions of service.
(3) No member of the staff of the Commissioner is to be regarded –
(a) as the servant or agent of the Crown, or
(b) as enjoying any status, immunity or privilege of the Crown.

Delegation

4 The Commissioner may authorise any member of his staff or the Deputy Commissioner to carry out any of his functions.

Pensions

5 (1) Schedule 1 to the Superannuation Act 1972 (c. 11) (kinds of employment and offices to which a scheme under section 1 of that Act may apply) is amended as set out in sub-paragraphs (2) and (3).
(2) At the end of the list headed 'Other Bodies' insert –
'Employment as a member of the staff of the Commissioner for Victims and Witnesses.'
(3) In the list headed 'Offices', in the appropriate places, insert –
'Commissioner for Victims and Witnesses.'
'Deputy Commissioner for Victims and Witnesses.'
(4) The Secretary of State must pay to the Minister for the Civil Service, at such times as the Minister for the Civil Service may direct, such sums as the Minister for the Civil Service may determine in respect of the increase attributable to sub-paragraphs (1) to (3) in the sums payable out of money provided by Parliament under the Superannuation Act 1972.

Finance

6 The Secretary of State must pay –

(a) the remuneration of the Commissioner and the Deputy Commissioner;
(b) such sums as he thinks fit in respect of the expenses of the Commissioner and the Deputy Commissioner.

Accounts

7 (1) The Commissioner must –

(a) keep proper accounts and proper records in relation to the accounts;
(b) prepare a statement of accounts in respect of each financial year, in the form directed by the Secretary of State;
(c) send copies of the statement to the Secretary of State and the Comptroller and Auditor General, not later than the 31 August following the end of the financial year to which it relates.

(2) The Comptroller and Auditor General must –

(a) examine, certify and report on the statement of accounts;
(b) lay copies of the statement and of his report before Parliament.

Annual plan

8 (1) The Commissioner must, before the beginning of each financial year apart from the first, prepare a plan setting out how he intends to exercise his functions during the financial year (an annual plan).

(2) In preparing the plan, the Commissioner must consider whether to deal in the plan with any issues specified by the Secretary of State.

(3) The Commissioner must send a copy of the plan to the Secretary of State for his approval.

(4) The Secretary of State must consult the Attorney General and the Lord Chancellor in deciding whether to approve the plan.

(5) If the Secretary of State does not approve the plan –

(a) he must give the Commissioner his reasons for not approving it, and
(b) the Commissioner must revise the plan.

(6) Sub-paragraphs (2) to (5) apply to a revised plan as they apply to the plan as first prepared.

Annual report

9 (1) The Commissioner must, as soon as possible after the end of each financial year, prepare a report on how he has exercised his functions during the financial year.

(2) The report for any financial year apart from the first must include –

(a) the Commissioner's annual plan for the financial year, and
(b) an assessment of the extent to which the plan has been carried out.

(3) The Commissioner must send a copy of the report to –

(a) the Secretary of State,
(b) the Attorney General, and
(c) the Lord Chancellor.

(4) The Secretary of State must –
   (a) lay a copy of the report before Parliament;
   (b) arrange for the report to be published.

Disqualification Acts

10 (1) In Part 3 of Schedule 1 to the House of Commons Disqualification Act 1975 (c. 24) (offices the holders of which are disqualified) at the appropriate places insert –

'Commissioner for Victims and Witnesses.'
'Deputy Commissioner for Victims and Witnesses.'

(2) In Part 3 of Schedule 1 to the Northern Ireland Assembly Disqualification Act 1975 (c. 25) (offices the holders of which are disqualified) at the appropriate places insert –

'Commissioner for Victims and Witnesses.'
'Deputy Commissioner for Victims and Witnesses.'

Meaning of 'financial year'

11 In this Schedule 'financial year' means –
   (a) the period beginning on the day on which section 48 comes into force and ending on the next 31 March (which is the first financial year), and
   (b) each subsequent period of 12 months beginning on 1 April.

SCHEDULE 9 AUTHORITIES WITHIN COMMISSIONER'S REMIT

Section 53

Government departments

1 The Department for Constitutional Affairs.
2 The Department for Education and Skills.
3 The Department of Health.
4 The Department of Trade and Industry.
5 The Department for Transport.
6 The Department for Work and Pensions.
7 The Foreign and Commonwealth Office.
8 The Home Office.
9 The Office of the Deputy Prime Minister.

Customs and Excise

10 The Commissioners of Customs and Excise.

Police forces etc

11 A police force for a police area in England or Wales.
12 The Serious Fraud Office.
13 The National Criminal Intelligence Service.
14 The National Crime Squad.

15 The force of constables appointed under section 53 of the British Transport Commission Act 1949 (c. xxix).
16 The Ministry of Defence Police.

Criminal injuries compensation

17 The Criminal Injuries Compensation Appeals Panel.
18 The Criminal Injuries Compensation Authority.

Health and safety

19 The Health and Safety Commission.
20 The Health and Safety Executive.

Legal services

21 The Legal Services Commission.

Court administration

22 Persons exercising functions relating to the carrying on of the business of a court.

Criminal justice system

23 The Criminal Cases Review Commission.
24 The Crown Prosecution Service.
25 A local probation board established under section 4 of the Criminal Justice and Court Services Act 2000 (c. 43).
26 The Parole Board.
27 The Prison Service.
28 The Youth Justice Board for England and Wales.
29 A youth offending team established under section 39 of the Crime and Disorder Act 1998 (c. 37).

Maritime and coastguards

30 The Maritime and Coastguard Agency.

SCHEDULE 10 MINOR AND CONSEQUENTIAL AMENDMENTS

Section 58(1)

Colonial Prisoners Removal Act 1884 (c. 31)

1 In section 10 of the Colonial Prisoners Removal Act 1884 (application of Act to removal of criminal lunatics), in subsection (3), in paragraph (a) for the words from 'give' to the end substitute 'by warrant direct that he is to be detained in such hospital, within the meaning given by section 145(1) of the Mental Health Act 1983, as may be specified in the direction; and any such direction shall have the same effect as a hospital order under section 37 of that Act together with a restriction order under section 41 of that Act, made without limitation of time;'.

Children and Young Persons Act 1933 (c. 12)

2 In Schedule 1 to the Children and Young Persons Act 1933 (offences against children and young persons with respect to which special provisions of the Act apply), after 'Infanticide' insert –

'An offence under section 5 of the Domestic Violence, Crime and Victims Act 2004, in respect of a child or young person.'

Criminal Procedure (Insanity) Act 1964 (c. 84)

3 In section 8(2) of the Criminal Procedure (Insanity) Act 1964 (interpretation), after the definition of 'duly approved' insert –

'"local probation board" means a local probation board established under section 4 of the Criminal Justice and Court Services Act 2000;'.

Criminal Appeal Act 1968 (c. 19)

4 In section 15 of the Criminal Appeal Act 1968 (right of appeal against finding of disability), in subsection (1), for the words 'the jury has returned' substitute 'there have been'.

5 In section 37 of that Act (detention of defendant on appeal by the Crown to House of Lords), in subsection (4), for paragraph (b) substitute –

'(b) a hospital order made by virtue of section 5(2)(a) of the Criminal Procedure (Insanity) Act 1964 (powers to deal with persons not guilty by reason of insanity or unfit to plead etc),'.

6 In section 51 of that Act (interpretation), in subsection (2A), for '6, 14 or 14A' substitute '6 or 14'.

Children and Young Persons Act (Northern Ireland) 1968 (c. 34 (N.I.))

7 In Schedule 1 to the Children and Young Persons Act (Northern Ireland) 1968 (offences against children and young persons with respect to which special provisions of the Act apply), after 'Infanticide' insert –

'An offence under section 5 of the Domestic Violence, Crime and Victims Act 2004, in respect of a child or young person.'

Juries Act 1974 (c. 23)

8 (1) Section 11 of the Juries Act 1974 (ballot and swearing of jurors) is amended as follows.

(2) In subsection (5) omit paragraph (b).

(3) In subsection (6) omit ', (b)'.

Rehabilitation of Offenders Act 1974 (c. 53)

9 In section 1(3) of the Rehabilitation of Offenders Act 1974 (meaning of 'sentence' for the purposes of that Act), after 'other than' insert –

'(za) a surcharge imposed under section 161A of the Criminal Justice Act 2003;'.

Magistrates' Courts Act 1980 (c. 43)

10 In section 108 of the Magistrates' Courts Act 1980 (right of appeal to Crown Court), after subsection (3) insert –

'(4) Subsection (3)(d) above does not prevent an appeal against a surcharge imposed under section 161A of the Criminal Justice Act 2003.'

11 In section 139 of that Act (disposal of sums adjudged to be paid by conviction) –

(a) after paragraph (a) insert –

'(aa) in the second place in payment to the fund mentioned in paragraph (c) below of surcharges imposed under section 161A of the Criminal Justice Act 2003;';

(b) in paragraph (b), for 'second' substitute 'third'.

Criminal Appeal (Northern Ireland) Act 1980 (c. 47)

12 In section 13A of the Criminal Appeal (Northern Ireland) Act 1980 (appeal against finding of unfitness to be tried), in subsection (1), for 'the jury has returned' substitute 'there has been'.

13 In section 19(1A)(a) of that Act (legal aid), after 'appeal under' insert ' section 18A of the Domestic Violence, Crime and Victims Act 2004,'.

Supreme Court Act 1981 (c. 54)

14 In section 55 of the Supreme Court Act 1981 (constitution of criminal division of Court of Appeal), in subsection (4)(a)(iii) omit the words 'of a jury'.

15 In section 81 of that Act (power of Crown Court to grant bail), in subsection (1A), for 'or 15' substitute ', 15 or 16A'.

Criminal Justice Act 1982 (c. 48)

16 In Schedule 1 to the Criminal Justice Act 1982 (offences excluded from early release provisions), in Part 2, after the entry relating to the Sexual Offences Act 2003 (c. 42) insert –

'*Domestic Violence, Crime and Victims Act 2004*
Section 5 (causing or allowing the death of a child or vulnerable adult).'

Representation of the People Act 1983 (c. 2)

17 In section 3A of the Representation of the People Act 1983 (disenfranchisement of offenders detained in mental hospitals), for subsection (5) substitute –

'(5) As respects any part of the United Kingdom, this section applies to any person in respect of whom a hospital order has been made by virtue of –

(a) section 116A of the Army Act 1955 or the Air Force Act 1955 or section 63A of the Naval Discipline Act 1957, or
(b) section 16 or 23 of the Courts-Martial (Appeals) Act 1968.'

Mental Health Act 1983 (c. 20)

18 In section 47 of the Mental Health Act 1983 (removal to hospital of persons serving sentences of imprisonment, etc), in subsection (5)(a), for the words 'under any

enactment to which section 46 applies' substitute 'made in consequence of a finding of insanity or unfitness to stand trial'.

19 In section 69 of that Act (application to tribunals concerning patients subject to hospital orders etc), in subsection (2)(a) –

(a) for 'below,' substitute 'below or';
(b) omit 'or section 5(1) of the Criminal Procedure (Insanity) Act 1964'.

20 In section 71 of that Act (references by Home Secretary concerning restricted patients) omit subsections (5) and (6).

21 In section 79 of that Act (interpretation of Part 5), in subsection (1) –

(a) for paragraph (a) substitute –

'(a) is treated by virtue of any enactment as subject to a hospital order and a restriction order; or';

(b) omit paragraph (b).

22 In section 84 of that Act (removal to England and Wales of offenders found insane in Channel Islands and Isle of Man), in subsection (2), for the words from 'had been' to the end substitute 'were subject to a hospital order together with a restriction order, made without limitation of time'.

23 (1) Schedule 5 to that Act (transitional and saving provisions) is amended as follows.
(2) For paragraph 21 substitute –

'21. Any direction to which section 71(4) of the Mental Health Act 1959 applied immediately before the commencement of this Act shall have the same effect as a hospital order together with a restriction order, made without limitation of time.'

(3) In paragraph 37(2), for 'direction under section 46 of this Act' substitute 'hospital order together with a restriction order, made without limitation of time'.

Police and Criminal Evidence Act 1984 (c. 60)

24 In Schedule 5 to the Police and Criminal Evidence Act 1984 (serious arrestable offences), in Part 2, after paragraph 23 insert –

'Domestic Violence, Crime and Victims Act 2004

24 Section 5 (causing or allowing the death of a child or vulnerable adult).'

Prosecution of Offences Act 1985 (c. 23)

25 In section 16 of the Prosecution of Offences Act 1985 (defence costs), in subsection (4) (power of Court of Appeal to make defendant's costs order), after paragraph (c) insert 'or

(d) allows, to any extent, an appeal under section 16A of that Act (appeal against order made in cases of insanity or unfitness to plead);'.

Coroners Act 1988 (c. 13)

26 In section 16 of the Coroners Act 1988 (adjournment of inquest in event of criminal proceedings), in subsection (1)(a), after sub-paragraph (iii) insert –

'(iv) an offence under section 5 of the Domestic Violence, Crime and Victims Act 2004 (causing or allowing the death of a child or vulnerable adult); or'.

27 In section 17 of that Act (coroner to be informed of result of criminal proceedings), in subsections (1) and (2), at the end of paragraph (c) insert '; or

(d) an offence under section 5 of the Domestic Violence, Crime and Victims Act 2004 (causing or allowing the death of a child or vulnerable adult),'.

Criminal Justice Act 1988 (c. 33)

28 In section 41 of the Criminal Justice Act 1988 (power of Crown Court to deal with summary offence where person committed for either way offence), after subsection (4) insert –

'(4A) The committal of a person under this section in respect of an offence to which section 40 above applies shall not prevent him being found guilty of that offence under section 6(3) of the Criminal Law Act 1967 (alternative verdicts on trial on indictment); but where he is convicted under that provision of such an offence, the functions of the Crown Court under this section in relation to the offence shall cease.'

Police and Criminal Evidence (Northern Ireland) Order 1989 (S.I. 1989/1341 (N.I. 12))

29 In Schedule 5 to the Police and Criminal Evidence (Northern Ireland) Order 1989 (serious arrestable offences), in Part 2, after paragraph 14 insert –

'Domestic Violence, Crime and Victims Act 2004

15 Section 5 (causing or allowing the death of a child or vulnerable adult).'

Criminal Justice Act 1991 (c. 53)

30 In section 24 of the Criminal Justice Act 1991 (recovery of fines etc by deductions from income support), after subsection (3) insert –

'(3A) This section applies in relation to a surcharge imposed under section 161A of the Criminal Justice Act 2003 as if any reference in subsection (1) or (3) above to a fine included a reference to a surcharge.'

Criminal Appeal Act 1995 (c. 35)

31 In section 9 of the Criminal Appeal Act 1995 (references by Criminal Cases Review Commission to Court of Appeal), in subsection (6), for the words 'a jury in England and Wales has returned' substitute 'in England and Wales there have been'.

32 In section 10 of that Act (which makes equivalent provision for Northern Ireland), in subsection (7), for the words 'a jury in Northern Ireland has returned' substitute 'in Northern Ireland there has been'.

Law Reform (Year and a Day Rule) Act 1996 (c. 19)

33 In section 2 of the Law Reform (Year and a Day Rule) Act 1996 (restriction on institution of proceedings for fatal offence), in subsection (3), at the end of paragraph (b) insert ', or

(c) an offence under section 5 of the Domestic Violence, Crime and Victims Act 2004 (causing or allowing the death of a child or vulnerable adult).'

Family Law Act 1996 (c. 27)

34 (1) Section 36 of the Family Law Act 1996 (one cohabitant or former cohabitant with no existing right to occupy) is amended as follows.

(2) In subsection (1)(c), for the words from 'live together as' to the end substitute 'cohabit or a home in which they at any time cohabited or intended to cohabit'.

(3) In subsection (6)(f), for 'lived together as husband and wife' substitute 'cohabited'.

35 In section 38 of that Act (neither cohabitant or former cohabitant entitled to occupy), in subsection (1)(a), for 'live or lived together as husband and wife' substitute 'cohabit or cohabited'.

36 (1) Section 42 of that Act (non-molestation orders) is amended as follows.

(2) After subsection (4) insert –

'(4A) A court considering whether to make an occupation order shall also consider whether to exercise the power conferred by subsection (2)(b).

(4B) In this Part "the applicant", in relation to a non-molestation order, includes (where the context permits) the person for whose benefit such an order would be or is made in exercise of the power conferred by subsection (2)(b).'

(3) In subsection (5)(a) omit the words from 'or' to 'made'.

37 (1) Section 46 of that Act (undertakings) is amended as follows.

(2) In subsection (3), after 'under subsection (1)' insert 'instead of making an occupation order'.

(3) After that subsection insert –

'(3A) The court shall not accept an undertaking under subsection (1) instead of making a non-molestation order in any case where it appears to the court that –

(a) the respondent has used or threatened violence against the applicant or a relevant child; and

(b) for the protection of the applicant or child it is necessary to make a non-molestation order so that any breach may be punishable under section 42A.'

(4) In subsection (4), for 'it were an order of the court' substitute 'the court had made an occupation order or a non-molestation order in terms corresponding to those of the undertaking'.

38 (1) Section 47 of that Act (arrest for breach of occupation order or non-molestation order) is amended as follows.

(2) Omit subsection (1).

(3) In subsections (2) and (4), for 'a relevant order' substitute 'an occupation order'.

(4) In subsections (3) and (5), for 'the relevant order' substitute 'the occupation order'.

(5) In subsection (8), for the words up to the end of paragraph (b) substitute –

'If the court –

(a) has made a non-molestation order, or

(b) has made an occupation order but has not attached a power of arrest under subsection (2) or (3) to any provision of the order, or has attached that power only to certain provisions of the order,'.

39 In section 49 of that Act (variation and discharge of orders), in subsection (4) omit 'or non-molestation order'.

40 In section 62 of that Act (definitions), in subsection (1)(b), for '"former cohabitants" is to be read accordingly, but' substitute '"cohabit" and "former cohabitants" are to be read accordingly, but the latter expression'.

41 (1) In section 63 of that Act (interpretation of Part 4), subsection (1) is amended as follows.
(2) At the beginning of the definition of 'cohabitant' and 'former cohabitant' insert '"cohabit",'.
(3) In the definition of 'relative' –
(a) for 'or nephew' in paragraph (b) substitute ', nephew or first cousin';
(b) for 'is living or has lived with another person as husband and wife' substitute 'is cohabiting or has cohabited with another person'.

42 (1) Schedule 7 to that Act (transfer of certain tenancies on divorce etc or on separation of cohabitants) is amended as follows.
(2) In paragraph 3(2), for 'to live together as husband and wife' substitute 'to cohabit'.
(3) In paragraph 4(b), for 'lived together as husband and wife' substitute 'cohabited'.

Protection from Harassment Act 1997 (c. 40)

43 (1) Section 5 of the Protection from Harassment Act 1997 (power to make restraining order where defendant convicted of offence under section 2 or 4 of that Act) is amended as follows.
(2) In the heading, at the end insert '**on conviction**'.
(3) In subsection (2) omit 'further'.

44 In section 7 of that Act (interpretation), in subsection (1), for 'sections 1 to 5' substitute 'sections 1 to 5A'.

Crime (Sentences) Act 1997 (c. 43)

45 (1) Section 47 of the Crime (Sentences) Act 1997 (power to specify hospital units) is amended as follows.
(2) Omit subsections (1)(d) and (2)(c).
(3) For subsection (4) substitute –
'(4) A reference in this section to section 37 or 41 of the 1983 Act includes a reference to that section as it applies by virtue of –
(a) section 5 of the Criminal Procedure (Insanity) Act 1964,
(b) section 6 or 14 of the Criminal Appeal Act 1968,
(c) section 116A of the Army Act 1955 or the Air Force Act 1955 or section 63A of the Naval Discipline Act 1957, or
(d) section 16 or 23 of the Courts-Martial (Appeals) Act 1968.'

46 (1) Schedule 1 to that Act (transfers of prisoners within the British Islands) (as amended by Schedule 32 to the Criminal Justice Act 2003) is amended as follows.
(2) In paragraph 8 (restricted transfers from England and Wales to Scotland), in sub-paragraphs (2)(a) and (4)(a), for '264' substitute '264A'.
(3) In paragraph 9 (restricted transfers from England and Wales to Northern Ireland), in sub-paragraphs (2)(a) and (4)(a), for '264' substitute '264A'.

Protection from Harassment (Northern Ireland) Order 1997 (S.I. 1997/1180 (N.I. 9))

47 (1) Article 7 of the Protection from Harassment (Northern Ireland) Order 1997 (power to make restraining order where defendant convicted of offence under Article 4 or 6 of that Act) is amended as follows.

(2) In the heading, at the end insert '**on conviction**'.

(3) In paragraph (2) omit 'further'.

Crime and Disorder Act 1998 (c. 37)

48 In section 32 of the Crime and Disorder Act 1998 (racially or religiously aggravated harassment etc) omit subsection (7) (which is superseded by provision made by section 12(1) above).

Powers of Criminal Courts (Sentencing) Act 2000 (c. 6)

49 In section 132 of the Powers of Criminal Courts (Sentencing) Act 2000 (compensation orders: appeals etc), after subsection (4) insert –

'(4A) Where an order is made in respect of a person under subsection (3) or (4) above, the Court of Appeal or House of Lords shall make such order for the payment of a surcharge under section 161A of the Criminal Justice Act 2003, or such variation of the order of the Crown Court under that section, as is necessary to secure that the person's liability under that section is the same as it would be if he were being dealt with by the Crown Court.'

50 In section 136 of that Act (power to order statement as to financial circumstances of parent or guardian), in subsection (1), for 'or compensation' substitute ', compensation or surcharge'.

51 (1) Section 137 of that Act (power to order parent or guardian to pay fine, costs or compensation) is amended as follows.

(2) In the heading, for '**or compensation**' substitute '**, compensation or surcharge**'.

(3) After subsection (1) insert –

'(1A) Where but for this subsection a court would order a child or young person to pay a surcharge under section 161A of the Criminal Justice Act 2003, the court shall order that the surcharge be paid by the parent or guardian of the child or young person instead of by the child or young person himself, unless the court is satisfied –

(a) that the parent or guardian cannot be found; or

(b) that it would be unreasonable to make an order for payment, having regard to the circumstances of the case.'

(4) In subsection (3), for 'subsections (1) and (2)' substitute 'subsections (1) to (2)'.

52 (1) Section 138 of that Act (fixing of fine or compensation to be paid by parent or guardian) is amended as follows.

(2) In the heading, for '**or compensation**' substitute '**, compensation or surcharge**'.

(3) Before paragraph (a) of subsection (1) insert –

'(za) subsection (3) of section 161A of the Criminal Justice Act 2003 (surcharges) and subsection (4A) of section 164 of that Act (fixing of fines) shall have effect as if any reference in those subsections to the offender's means were a reference to those of the parent or guardian;'.

53 In section 142(1) of that Act (power of Crown Court to order search of persons before it) –

(a) before paragraph (a) insert –

'(za) the Crown Court orders a person to pay a surcharge under section 161A of the Criminal Justice Act 2003,';

(b) in paragraph (d), for 'or compensation' substitute ', compensation or surcharge'.

Criminal Justice and Court Services Act 2000 (c. 43)

54 The Criminal Justice and Court Services Act 2000 is amended as follows.

55 Section 69 (duties in connection with victims of certain offences) (which is superseded by section 35 of this Act) is repealed.

56 In Schedule 4 (offences against children for the purposes of disqualification orders), in paragraph 3, after paragraph (sa) insert –

'(sb) he commits an offence under section 5 of the Domestic Violence, Crime and Victims Act 2004 (causing or allowing the death of a child or vulnerable adult) in respect of a child.'

Sexual Offences Act 2003 (c. 42)

57 (1) Section 133 of the Sexual Offences Act 2003 (general interpretation of Part 2) is amended as follows.

(2) In subsection (1) –

(a) in the definition of 'admitted to a hospital', for paragraph (c) substitute –

'(c) section 46 of the Mental Health Act 1983, section 69 of the Mental Health (Scotland) Act 1984 or Article 52 of the Mental Health (Northern Ireland) Order 1986;';

(b) in the definition of 'detained in a hospital', for paragraph (c) substitute –

'(c) section 46 of the Mental Health Act 1983, section 69 of the Mental Health (Scotland) Act 1984 or Article 52 of the Mental Health (Northern Ireland) Order 1986;';

(c) in the definition of 'restriction order', for paragraph (c) substitute –

'(c) a direction under section 46 of the Mental Health Act 1983, section 69 of the Mental Health (Scotland) Act 1984 or Article 52 of the Mental Health (Northern Ireland) Order 1986;'.

(3) After that subsection insert –

'(1A) A reference to a provision specified in paragraph (a) of the definition of "admitted to a hospital", "detained in a hospital" or "restriction order" includes a reference to the provision as it applies by virtue of –

(a) section 5 of the Criminal Procedure (Insanity) Act 1964,
(b) section 6 or 14 of the Criminal Appeal Act 1968,
(c) section 116A of the Army Act 1955 or the Air Force Act 1955 or section 63A of the Naval Discipline Act 1957, or
(d) section 16 or 23 of the Courts-Martial (Appeals) Act 1968.'

58 In section 135 of that Act (interpretation: mentally disordered offenders), omit subsection (4)(c).

59 (1) Schedule 5 to that Act (other offences for the purposes of sexual offences prevention orders) is amended as follows.

(2) After paragraph 63 insert –

'63A An offence under section 5 of the Domestic Violence, Crime and Victims Act 2004 (causing or allowing the death of a child or vulnerable adult).'

(3) After paragraph 171 insert –

'171A An offence under section 5 of the Domestic Violence, Crime and Victims Act 2004 (causing or allowing the death of a child or vulnerable adult).'

(4) In paragraph 172, for '63' substitute '63A'.

Criminal Justice Act 2003 (c. 44)

60 In section 48 of the Criminal Justice Act 2003 (c. 44) (further provisions about trial without a jury), in subsection (6), for paragraphs (a) and (b) substitute 'the requirement under section 4A of the Criminal Procedure (Insanity) Act 1964 that any question, finding or verdict mentioned in that section be determined, made or returned by a jury'.

61 In section 50 of that Act (application of Part 7 to Northern Ireland), in subsection (13), for paragraphs (a) to (c) substitute –

'(a) for "section 4A of the Criminal Procedure (Insanity) Act 1964" substitute "Article 49A of the Mental Health (Northern Ireland) Order 1986", and

(b) for "that section" substitute "that Article".'

62 In section 74 of that Act (interpretation of Part 9), after subsection (6) insert –

'(7) In its application to a trial on indictment in respect of which an order under section 17(2) of the Domestic Violence, Crime and Victims Act 2004 has been made, this Part is to have effect with such modifications as the Secretary of State may by order specify.'

63 In section 151 of that Act (community order for persistent offender previously fined), in subsection (5), after 'compensation order' insert 'or a surcharge under section 161A'.

64 In section 305 of that Act (interpretation of Part 12), in subsection (1), insert at the appropriate place –

'"compensation order" has the meaning given by section 130(1) of the Sentencing Act;'.

65 In Schedule 15 to that Act (specified offences for the purposes of Chapter 5 of Part 12 of that Act), in Part 1 (specified violent offences), after paragraph 63 insert –

'63A An offence under section 5 of the Domestic Violence, Crime and Victims Act 2004 (causing or allowing the death of a child or vulnerable adult).'

66 In Schedule 17 to that Act (Northern Ireland offences specified for the purposes of section 229(4)), in Part 1 (specified violent offences), after paragraph 60 insert –

'60A An offence under section 5 of the Domestic Violence, Crime and Victims Act 2004 (causing or allowing the death of a child or vulnerable adult).'

SCHEDULE 11 REPEAL

Section 58(2)

Short title and chapter	*Extent of repeal*
Criminal Procedure (Insanity) Act 1964 (c. 84)	Section 7. In section 8 – (a) the proviso to subsection (3); (b) in subsection (4), the words from ', except' to 'courts-martial,'. Schedule 2.
Criminal Appeal Act 1968 (c. 19)	Section 14A.
Courts-Martial (Appeals) Act 1968 (c. 20)	In Schedule 3, paragraph 3(b).

Short title and chapter	*Extent of repeal*
Juries Act 1974 (c. 23)	In section 11, paragraph (b) of subsection (5) and '(b)' in subsection (6). In Schedule 1, paragraph 4(2).
Supreme Court Act 1981 (c. 54)	In section 55(4)(a)(iii), the words 'of a jury'.
Mental Health Act 1983 (c. 20)	In section 69(2)(a), the words 'or section 5(1) of the Criminal Procedure (Insanity) Act 1964'. Section 71(5) and (6). Section 79(1)(b).
Prosecution of Offences Act 1985 (c. 23)	In section 16(4), the word 'or' preceding paragraph (c).
Coroners Act 1988 (c. 13)	In section 16(1)(a), the word 'or' preceding sub-paragraph (iii). In section 17, in subsections (1) and (2) the word 'or' preceding paragraph (c).
Criminal Procedure (Insanity and Unfitness to Plead) Act 1991 (c.25)	Sections 3 and 5. In section 6 (a) the definition of 'local probation board' in subsection (1); (b) subsection (2). Schedules 1 and 2.
Law Reform (Year and a Day Rule) Act 1996 (c.19)	In section 2(3), the word 'or' preceding paragraph (b).
Family Law Act 1996 (c. 27)	Section 41. In section 42(5)(a), the words from 'or' to 'made'. Section 47(1). In section 49(4), the words 'or non-molestation order'.
Armed Forces Act 1996 (c.46)	Section 8. Schedule 2.
Protection from Harassment Act 1997 (c.40)	In section 5, the words 'under section 2 or 4' in subsection (1) and the word 'further' in subsection (2).
Crime (Sentences) Act 1997 (c.43)	In section 47 (a) in subsection (1), paragraph (d) and the word 'or' preceding it; (b) in subsection (2), paragraph (c) and the word 'and' preceding it.
Protection from Harassment (Northern Ireland) Order 1997 (S.I.1997/1180 (N.I.9))	In Article 7, the words 'under Article 4 or 6' in paragraph (1) and the word 'further' in paragraph (2).
Crime and Disorder Act 1998 (c.37)	Section 32(7).
Access to Justice Act 1999 (c.22)	In Schedule 13, paragraph 163.
Powers of Criminal Courts (Sentencing) Act 2000 (c.6)	In Schedule 9, paragraph 133.
Care Standards Act 2000 (c.14)	In Schedule 4, paragraph 16.

Short title and chapter	*Extent of repeal*
Criminal Justice and Court Services Act 2000 (c.43)	Section 69. In Schedule 7, paragraphs 99 to 102.
Sexual Offences Act 2003 (c. 42)	Section 135(4)(c).
Criminal Justice Act 2003 (c.44)	In section 246(6), in the definition of 'the required custodial days', the word 'or' preceding paragraph (b). In section 264(1), the word 'and' preceding paragraph (b).

SCHEDULE 12 TRANSITIONAL AND TRANSITORY PROVISIONS

Section 59

1 (1) Section 1 and paragraphs 37 to 39 of Schedule 10 apply only in relation to conduct occurring on or after the commencement of that section.

(2) In relation to an offence committed before the commencement of section 154(1) of the Criminal Justice Act 2003 (c. 44), the reference to 12 months in subsection (5)(b) of section 42A of the Family Law Act 1996 (inserted by section 1 of this Act) is to be read as a reference to six months.

2 In section 5, the reference in subsection (1)(a) to an unlawful act does not include an act that (or so much of an act as) occurs before the commencement of that section.

3 (1) This paragraph has effect, in relation to any time before the commencement of the repeal (by paragraph 51 of Schedule 3 to the Criminal Justice Act 2003) of section 6 of the Magistrates' Courts Act 1980 (c. 43), where –

(a) a magistrates' court is considering under subsection (1) of that section whether to commit a person ('the accused') for trial for an offence of murder or manslaughter, and

(b) the accused is charged in the same proceedings with an offence under section 5 above in respect of the same death.

(2) If there is sufficient evidence to put the accused on trial by jury for the offence under section 5, there is deemed to be sufficient evidence to put him on trial by jury for the offence of murder or manslaughter.

4 Section 10 applies only in relation to offences committed on or after the commencement of that section.

5 (1) Section 12(1) and paragraphs 43(3) and 48 of Schedule 10 do not apply where the conviction occurs before the commencement of those provisions.

(2) Section 12(2) applies only in relation to applications made on or after the commencement of that provision.

(3) Section 12(4) and paragraphs 43(2) and 44 of Schedule 10 do not apply where the acquittal (or, where subsection (5) of the inserted section 5A applies, the allowing of the appeal) occurs before the commencement of those provisions.

6 (1) Section 13(1) and paragraph 47(3) of Schedule 10 do not apply where the conviction occurs before the commencement of those provisions.

(2) Section 13(2) applies only in relation to applications made on or after the commencement of that provision.

(3) Section 13(4) and paragraph 47(2) of Schedule 10 do not apply where the acquittal (or, where paragraph (5) of the inserted Article 7A applies, the allowing of the appeal) occurs before the commencement of those provisions.

7 Section 14 applies only in relation to offences committed on or after the commencement of that section.

8 (1) The provisions mentioned in sub-paragraph (2) do not apply –

(a) in relation to proceedings before the Crown Court or a court-martial, where the accused was arraigned before the commencement of those provisions;

(b) in relation to proceedings before the Court of Appeal or the Courts-Martial Appeal Court, where the hearing of the appeal began before that commencement.

(2) The provisions are –

(a) sections 22 and 23;

(b) section 24 and Schedule 2;

(c) section 26 and Schedule 3;

(d) paragraphs 5, 6, 8, 17 to 21, 45, 60 and 61 of Schedule 10

9 The Schedule inserted by Schedule 2 has effect in relation to any time before the commencement of sections 8 and 37 of the Courts Act 2003 (c. 39) –

(a) as if a reference to a local justice area were to a petty sessions area;

(b) as if a reference to a designated officer were to a justices' chief executive.

10 Each entry in Schedule 11 applies in the same way as the provision of this Act to which it corresponds.

INDEX